Play Lightly

on the Earth

Nature Activities for
Children
Ages 3 to 9

BY JACQUELINE HORSFALL

DAWN Publications

DEDICATION

For all my friends "feathered, furred and fingered"
at Spencer Crest Nature Center. —JH

Publisher's Cataloging-in-Publication
(Provided by Quality Books, Inc.)

Horsfall, Jacqueline.
    Play lightly on the earth / Jacqueline Horsfall. –1st ed.

    p. cm.
    ISBN: 1-883220-68-8

    Nature study—Activity programs.   I. Title.
    LB1130.5.S35H67 1997   372.3'57
                                       QBI97-40607

Published by DAWN Publications
14618 Tyler Foote Road
Nevada City, CA 95959
(530) 478-7540

Printed in Canada

10 9 8 7 6 5 4 3 2 1
First Edition

Design by LeeAnn Brook
Illustrations by Sarah Brink
Computer Layout by Rob Froelick
Photograph by Rodney Polden (page 18)
Photographs by John Hendrickson (cover, pages
35, 40 47, 52, 66, 73, 94, 105, 108, 132, 144, 151)
Photographs by Scott Chantland (pages 27, 31, 45,
61, 79, 91, 113, 119, 121, 155)
"Down Under My Feet" and "A Week at Camp" by
Jacqueline Horsfall reprinted by permission of the
Children's Better Health Institute, Benjamin
Franklin Literary & Medical Society, Inc.

Contents

Dear Reader,

I call this book my "vegetable soup," a stewpot full of activities which have been slowly simmering in my mind for my 15 years of involvement in nature center youth programs.

The word *vegetable* means at root *to grow, animate, invigorate, enliven.* Every so often, I tossed a fresh vegetable—an invigorating idea—into the soup after observing children in outdoor learning situations. I stirred in my own mental notes about what fascinated kids (anything gross, alive, or touchable), what totally bored them (too much talk), and when to move on (poking friends, fiddling with zippers). I sprinkled in the wisdom of pre-schoolers who make startling, intelligent observations about life processes, like this one: "If I eat this seed and poop it out, it might grow into a tree." (An actual method of seed dispersal by animals.) I seasoned the broth with concerns from parents and group leaders who expressed interest in educating their own children outdoors "if I only knew more science," unaware that their own enthusiasm and good examples outweighed any deficiencies in book learning. Throughout this slow cooking process, one ingredient remained constant: the deep concern kids have for the health and welfare of the planet they will inherit from us.

The flavorful ideas blended nicely and finally bubbled up into a concoction of poems, activities and guided imagery exercises with no-fuss guidance for you, the adult. Some of the activities are timeless old favorites; others are fresh ideas of my own creation, out of my own experience.

Try them all. There's nothing so forlorn as a pot of soup that hasn't been sampled. And there's nothing quite so inviting as a pot in constant use, with all the noise, mess, antics and intimacy of a crowd of hungry young minds in the kitchen.

Happy tasting,

Jackie

Introduction

Heads, Hearts & Hands-On

"Hey, look!" piped a snow-suited first grader. She pointed to a patch of color beneath the pine boughs. "A blue woodpecker!" Her classmates swarmed around to check out the highlight of their field trip.

I crouched down and swept the lifeless body out into the open. "It's not a woodpecker," I announced. "It's a blue jay."

"Yeah, it's a *dead* blue jay," echoed a voice from the group.

"Can I take it home?" asked another.

"Let's just leave the jay under the tree and let nature take care of it," I said, sliding the bird's body across the snow and back under the pine. "It's time to get back."

As we started down the trail to the nature center, I felt a tug on my parka. The tiny girl stared up at me, a mittened hand swiping her runny nose.

"*Maybe* it's a blue jay," she said agreeably, "but it sure looks like a woodpecker to me."

Years later, I realized that she was right. While casually paging through a field guide to North American birds, I was struck by the uncanny resemblance between crested woodpeckers and blue jays. Color aside, both sported long spike-sharp beaks and prominent crests, caps, or crowns. Even the distinctive black-and-white facial patterns were similar. One woodpecker species description actually used the term "jay-sized."

Yes, I had to admit it. That jay sure did look like a woodpecker. If only I had listened to my perceptive first-grader *with my imagination*, I might have spotted some of those similarities, too. In my haste to move the group along, and through my own inattentiveness, I missed the proffered cue and the chance for a meaningful exchange: "A blue woodpecker! This bird is known as a blue *jay*, but you've really got me wondering now . . . why do you think it looks like a woodpecker?"

When children speak, adults often forget to listen with their imaginations. Why do we forget? Because imagining demands absolute attention. It means wrapping oneself in the fascination of the sense world, oblivious to beeping pagers and pocket calendars. Imagining spurns time and demands the absorption of a child in intense play. (Thoreau's aunt complained that he could spend six hours watching frogs hatch.) Imagination sees the world in a creative, offbeat way, often not obvious to the pragmatic.

In her own imaginative way, my smart first-grader unknowingly used a basic form of ordering—finding *connecting patterns*—and noticed the similarities between woodpeckers and blue jays. Out of the mouths of babes! By recognizing patterns of interconnectedness among species, we have proof that the natural world is not a collection of separate "things" but a deep unfolding collaborative process.

So, let's listen to children with our imaginations. We'll spot some blue woodpeckers—and some inspiring young human companions—out there in the process.

Children are movers and shakers. They touch, poke, smell, dig, explore. They love to investigate mysteries and solve puzzles. Play is the very vehicle of their growth. Through this busy play, they uncover their world.

This activity book—or environmental play book—is designed for *children ages 3 - 9* and *accompanying adults (or responsible teenagers)*.

For 3- to 5-year-olds: The first years of a child's life are critically important to brain development. Don't underestimate your child's ability to understand basic scientific concepts. A pre-schooler can handle material geared for a higher age group *if presented in an imaginative way by an adult who expresses excitement about the topic.* Enthusiasm is contagious. Encourage your child's natural curiosity, and keep the experience upbeat, positive, and short.

For 6- to 9-year-olds: The emphasis is on creative thinking, problem-solving, and skill development—serious work all in the guise of play—and keeping them interested enough to go on learning on their own. This age group is open to teachable virtues: empathy and caring for wildlife, respect and responsibility for the Earth, resourcefulness, self-reliance, and cooperation among species.

The primary aim of outdoor education is to help children develop a respect for life by understanding how the Earth works and sustains itself. They can then integrate what they've learned into ways of thinking and acting responsibly.

Parents, grandparents, teachers, counselors, day care providers, and youth group leaders play a crucial role in educating good Earth citizens. Set a good example. Your words and actions won't go unnoticed. Children observe and remember your example far more than you may realize. Many children believe that grown-ups are destroying the Earth, and they don't buy our excuses for not changing our habits.

Teach your children (and yourself) how to play lightly on a small planet with limited resources, an exploding population, and a beauty so breathtaking that orbiting astronauts weep with joy.

How to Teach Effectively
When You Don't Know the Answers

So you don't have a science background? *Relax.* What's far more important is having an upbeat attitude about the outdoors.

To aid the nonscientist, activities are based on *simple* outdoor experiences, focusing on the diversity of nature. Concepts are briefly explained in easy-to-understand terms. Sample questions for discussion range from **Easy** to **Challenging**, with **Hints** provided for answering the head-scratching ones.

These questions will generate more questions, maybe more than you can answer comfortably. Let's face it—we adults don't know everything. Usually we're too ashamed to admit this to our children (until they become teenagers and find out for themselves). It's hard enough answering questions about love, life, and school, but trying to name and classify species and ecosystems is over the heads of most adults with non-science backgrounds. Don't be intimidated. Follow a few ground rules:

- *Read the section of each activity titled "The Inside Scoop."* You'll get an overview of the basic concept in story form (and save face when the "but *why?*" questions start flying).

- *Listen with your imagination.* Wipe "No, that's wrong" from your vocabulary. Instead, ask "Why do you think that?" Try to uncover the connection in the child's mind. The connection may have a basis in fact (blue woodpeckers) or fiction (dinosaurs eat people). Knowing the source and connection, you can gently clear up any misunderstanding.

- *Laugh.* Nature is full of humor. Prompt a thought with "What if . . ." and see where it leads. Kids are often struck silly in discussing "scat" (animal droppings). Carry it further. There's an easy lesson in pollution from asking the question, "What do you think would happen if *people* pooped wherever they wanted?" Kids have their own ideas—and they usually don't match scientific explanations.

- *Guide with questions rather than trying to name everything.* Although children often ask, "What's that?", they're not asking for mere labels as much as more information. Guide the child to find his or her own answer by asking other questions. "What's it doing?" "Is it alive?" "Why is it making that noise?" "What does it feel like when you touch it?"

The most important point to remember—one that will save you every time—is this: *A child asking "What's that?" is usually looking for more information, not a label.*

The same is true of you, too. Think about it. You're sitting at home alone, reading. The house is quiet. Suddenly you hear a rustling sound, like dried leaves, then a high-pitched squeal over the clatter of metal. You jump up in fright, gasping "What's that?" Are you really asking for the scientific name of the creature lurking near your house? Or are you asking for more specific information to piece together, leading to a logical conclusion: it's only the neighbor's cat tipping over your trash can.

If you can answer your child's question with a scientific name, great, but it's still not enough. It's most important to keep the experience flowing with observations such as these:

(Child, pointing) *What's that?*

 (Adult) Look what you found! What would you call that shape?

Round, like a ball.

You're right . . . do you think it's some kind of animal?

No way!

Why not?

It's growing right here on this plant. See the flowers?

Why don't you touch it. Is it soft or hard?

(Child touches plant) *Hard. I can't even squeeze it.*

Does it smell like a flower?

(Child sniffs plant) *It doesn't have a smell.*

Why do you think the ball grew on this plant?

Maybe it's sick.

Look around. Do you see other plants with lumps like this?

(Child checks other plants) *Here's one . . . and here . . . lots!*

See the hole in this ball. How do you suppose it got there?

Maybe a bird pecked it.

Good idea. How else?

Maybe a bug lives inside and the hole is the door.

That sounds good, too. Let's take one home. You can help me find out more about this ball when we go to the library (or nature center).

Notice how a definite answer is never given; instead, questions carry the conversation, using *sensations* and *common sense observations*. In this case, the observations led to a correct and logical conclusion. Later research will show that this was a **ball gall** found on goldenrod stems, formed by a small insect which uses the ball as its home. The hole in the gall might have been caused by a bird trying to break through to eat the larva, or from the insect itself as it matures and drills a hole from inside out.

Obviously, the name would not have satisfied the child's curiosity nor provided an intimate personal learning experience for both child and adult. Remember, no living or non-living thing on this planet had a name until humans began sorting and classifying. Experience in the natural world will always be primary.

- *Offer to find the information later.* That spark of curiosity can be re-kindled. Say, "I don't know right now . . . but we can find the answer together." Public libraries and nature centers have descriptive field guides. Librarians can point out juvenile science books on the subject. Call your local college or university and speak to an instructor in environmental or natural science. Check with your local Department of Environmental Conservation or county Cooperative Extension office. Encourage your child to research with you. The answer is out there.

Adults with science backgrounds should supplement these activities with their own specialized knowledge, keeping in mind that *experiencing, listening with imagination, finding humor*, and *guiding with questions* are important teaching tools—especially when you don't know all the answers.

How to Play Lightly

Select a style of exploration that fits your needs.

   1. The *casual* approach—Activities are stand-alone and may be done in any order, by individual child and adult, or in groups led by adults. This style may be preferable for parents, grandparents, and day care providers who want a spontaneous, one-time outdoor experience ("Hey, it's stopped raining! Let's go out and do something.") or for teachers under a time constraint. Simply thumb through the book and choose one (or more) activity to fit your time, place, and interest.

OR

   2. The *sequential* approach—Activities follow the Flow Learning™ method, a flexible nature awareness activity pattern designed by naturalist Joseph Cornell. This style is preferable for camp personnel, scout leaders, naturalists, home-schooling parents, and teachers who want to use activities in a purposeful, directional way. Each activity is marked with a symbol to help you plan a stimulating multi-activity program.

To make it easy for you to tell quickly what each game is like, each activity has a quick-reference symbol developed by Joseph Cornell; one of four animals, to indicate the basic mood of each game. The symbols and their meanings are as follows:

Awaken Enthusiasm   *Energetic/Playful*
The otter spends his days frolicking; the only animal that plays (constantly!) throughout adult life, he is nature's embodiment of exuberant fun.

Focus Attention   *Attentive/Observational*
The crow is an extremely alert and intelligent rascal, who's likely to be found keenly observing anything that's going on.

Direct Experience   *Calm/Experiential*
Bears are very curious, and lead solitary, quiet lives. Their temperament makes them a perfect symbol for deeply experiencing nature.

Share Inspiration   *Reflective/Sharing*
Dolphins are gregarious and altruistic creatures. They cooperate and care for one another, and they also appear to be conscious of other forms of life. Dolphins beautifully express the qualities of sharing and altruism.

These four symbols represent the four stages of Flow Learning™ which may be used sequentially to maximize a learning pattern that observant teachers will recognize as one that recurs naturally in the daily lives and activities of young children. See Appendix A for more information about the Flow Learning™ approach, how *Play Lightly* activities work in conjunction with the Flow Learning™ approach, and sample Flow Learning™ lessons.

Please note that some activities are seasonal or regional. Although all activities are geared for outdoor exploration, some may be adapted for indoor use (see Appendix B).

If you think a particular activity might scare your child (e.g., examining bugs), offer an alternative and let the child select one. ("We could check out some bugs today OR help birds build a nest.")

Adults should prepare *beforehand* by reading the **"The Inside Scoop."** This is background material for your own understanding of the topic. *Pass it on to your child in a way he or she can understand.* **Poems** and **Guided Visualizations** highlight each chapter's theme, offering quiet indoor/outdoor time to reflect and share thoughts.

If this book belongs to you, please mark it up! Highlight or underline, write comments in the margins, fold down the corners of important pages. Take this book with you when you're ready to move *outdoors*—where the real raw materials are located. Here's a sample activity format:

① *Title of activity listed in contents*

② *Flow learning quick-reference symbol for mood of the activity.*

③ *Activity objective.*

Home Improvement

Learn how birds actively ~ely build shelter to keep their ~ng young safe from predators and bad weather conditions

④ *Overview for adult. Explain to children in terms they can understand.*

> **The Inside Scoop:** When birds are building their nests in the spring, they fly around looking for nesting materials. A nest usually has a framework of twigs lined with softer materials such as fur and hair, moss, leaves, grass, bits of string. Some birds pluck their own feathers to make a fluffy lining. Humans can help birds build their homes by providing a place for "one-stop shopping."

Get ready!

⑤ *Gather materials indoors* AND →

⑥ *do this before starting out.*

Small woven basket with a handle OR net bag (the kind onions are sold in)
Scissors and ruler
Small pieces of yarn, string, fabric snips, dryer lint (*Do not* use sewing thread or fishing line)

Get set! ↘

Cut the yarn or string into pieces no longer than 4 inches.

Go!

⑦ *Outdoor discovery starts here.*

1. Search for more nesting materials outdoors: feathers, unraveled burlap, kite string, old shoelaces, dried grass, small twigs. Cut these to 4 inches or less.

2. Stuff the nesting materials inside your basket or bag. Let some pieces of yarn and string dangle outside.

3. Hang your basket or bag securely on a tree limb, post, fence, or outdoor plant hook, in plain sight for nest-building birds.

4. Watch for birds to pick up the dangling strings and fly away with them.

Let's talk

⑧ *Sample questions to ask during or after, arranged from easy to more challenging.*

What kinds of materials do birds use to build nests?
What do people use to build their homes?
Why do birds like yarn and string? Why do they like short pieces? What might happen with longer pieces? (*Hint: catch on tree limbs as bird is flying.*)
If you tracked a bird back to its nest, why do you think it built in that spot?
What's wrong with using sewing thread or fishing line? (*Hint: birds become tangled and can't fly.*)
Why should you be careful about throwing away plastic 6-pack rings? (*Hint: larger birds strangle when their heads catch in the holes.*)

Tips For Exploring Outdoors

Before:

- *Start small.* Start by exploring your yard, city park, vacant lot or grassy field. Many kids haven't been outdoors enough to feel at ease in a dark scary forest. Explain that "wildlife" is all around them—from spiders to snakes and squirrels. Their idea of wildlife may be tigers, elephants and gorillas they've seen at the zoo.
- *Know the area.* It's easy to become lost, even on clearly-marked trails. Mark off a territory by saying, "We won't go any farther than the white fence and the big pine tree." **Note to teachers and group leaders:** If you are under a time constraint, be sure to preview the area beforehand. For example, the activity "Snag Hotel" needs a dead tree to ensure a successful learning experience. You may want to "salt" areas with natural items (e.g., feathers, acorns, tracks) to give everyone a fair chance at discovery.
- *Cover yourself.* When you least expect it, mud appears. Make sure children wear appropriate clothing and footwear for the conditions, with sun protection.
- *Pack light.* Nothing beats a "fanny pack" for collecting nature items (although plastic zip-lock bags will do). For a quick "nature bracelet", wrap a strip of masking or packaging tape, *sticky-side out,* around the child's wrist. The tape will hold small, light finds.

During:

- *Stay close.* In guiding groups, a minimum of one adult per ten children is recommended. Have them work in pairs or small groups. On trail hikes, make sure one adult is the "head" and one is the "tail" to keep stragglers in line.
- *Quiet, please.* When searching for wildlife, walk slowly and quietly to avoid scaring them. Do not approach any animal that seems sick or is seen out of its normal foraging hours (e.g., raccoons, skunks, bats during the day). Keep a good distance from hives and nesting areas.
- *Let it be.* Studying insects often involves disturbing their homes (lifting a rock or board). Encourage children to "put the roof back on" the homes of bugs when they're finished observing.
- *Steady does it.* Binoculars are great for observing without disturbing, but they're often too heavy for little hands. Try this: seat your child on the ground, with knees up, elbows on knees. Open or close the binoculars on the hinge until perfectly aligned with the child's eyes. Show how to focus. This position provides a steady base for keeping objects in sight.

After:

- *Look me over.* Check for ticks and "stickers" like burdocks.
- *Replay.* Talk about what you've seen, read more about it, or draw pictures of the experience to refresh the memory.
- *Keep your promise.* If you offered to find the answer to a particularly tough question, DO IT.

Play Lightly...

In the Plant World

The Fat Garden Blues

I hoed a deep row in the warm dark earth
And scattered some earthworms around,
      Planted and seeded
      Watered and weeded
As sprouts poked their heads above ground.

    Now I'm sad, broken-hearted and blue
    When I see what my small garden grew:

        Piles of potatoes!
        Two-ton tomatoes!
        Eight-zillion zucchini!
        Plump peas and green beanies!

    Landslides of vegetables cover my head
    Sprouting from closets and under my bed,
    Veggies galore for a few brontosaurs —
    Won't somebody help? I can't eat any more!

When you hoe a deep row in the warm dark earth
Closely count every seed that you choose
      Or for breakfast you'll munch
      Toasted broccoli crunch —
And sing the summertime fat garden blues.

Leaf Lines

Identify symmetry in patterns of natural design

The Inside Scoop: A figure has **line symmetry** if it can be folded on a line to make halves that are mirrored images. Familiar examples include drawing the half-outline of a heart or paper doll on the fold of a piece of paper, cutting on the outline, and opening the paper to a full figure. Figures may have curved or straight parts, folded horizontally or vertically. Line symmetry occurs in nature and human-made architectural structures and designs (picturing the "fold" in your mind). Even the human skeleton has line symmetry.

Get ready!

4 sheets of construction paper, any color
Pencil and scissors
Deck of playing cards
Small rectangular mirror (without bound edge)

Get set!

Fold each paper once and draw a half-outline of each suit (diamond, heart, spade, club) on the fold.

Cut and open paper to show how matching halves form a full, symmetrical figure
Optional: Fold and cut a paper doll to show human symmetry.

Go!

1. Take your paper figures outdoors to use as examples of line symmetry.

2. Find a leaf, fern frond, or blade of grass. Fold it in half. See if both halves match. Fold your leaf other ways and check for symmetry. Hold your mirror perpendicular along the leaf's center to show reflected symmetry.

3. See if you can find leaves that *do not* have matching halves.

Let's talk

Do all leaves have matching sides?
Is your mirror-leaf symmetrical? Why?
Tear off a piece of leaf. What happens to symmetry?
Look down at your body. Do you have symmetry?
What else in nature has symmetry—even if you can't fold it in half? *(Hint: trees, snowflakes, acorns, pine cones, skeletons.)*
What good is symmetry in nature? *(Hint: makes the world beautifully balanced.)*
What people-built structures have line symmetry? *(Hint: door frames, windows, arches, bridges.)*

Lumps & Bumps

Find out how insects depend upon plants for food, shelter, and protection

The Inside Scoop: Galls are swellings on the leaves, stems, flowers and roots of plants. Insects, mites, fungi and bacteria live inside galls—eating their own houses from the inside. Galls usually start with a female fly, wasp or other insect. In late spring, she lays her eggs on or in a plant. After an egg hatches, the larva puts chemicals into the plant so that it grows around the insect, forming a protective "house" for the winter. It eats and grows. In spring, the adult fly breaks through the covering of its gall home and climbs out.

Get ready!   Small slicing or sawing tool

Get set!   Find a patch of goldenrod. (Galls develop on hundreds of other trees and plants, but goldenrod "ball galls" are easily identified.)

Go!

1. Look for a stem with a round swelling.

2. Look for holes in the swelling. This means that the insect has left OR another bird, small animal or other insect has broken into the gall and eaten the larva.

3. Carefully slice or saw through the gall and look inside. (NOTE: To avoid destroying the insect's home, an empty gall is preferable here, if possible.)

Let's talk

What shape is the gall? Is it hard or soft?

A gall is a house. Who lives in it?

How is a gall-house like your own house? How is it different?
    (Hint: no TV!)

What kind of animal might like to eat what's inside? *(Hint: wood-peckers, squirrels, mice.)*

How would an animal get to the food inside?

How do insects get inside the gall? *(Hint: the female picks out a tender spot on the plant and lays her eggs.)*

How do the insects survive inside the gall? *(Hint: by eating their house.)*

What do insects do when they leave their gall? *(Hint: Find a mate. If female, she lays her eggs on the goldenrod and the cycle repeats.)*

Prickles

*Learn about one way
plants defend themselves*

The Inside Scoop: Plants and animals are in competition—plants are food for animals, yet must defend themselves to survive. Plants have perfected different ways of defending themselves from leaf-eating animals: poisoning, stinging, burning the mouth, irritating the skin (poison ivy), and piercing the skin with spines. The thorns and spines of plants are actually stems or leaves which have evolved into protective devices. Sometimes leaves have spines along their veins and edges (thistle, holly); others arm their trunks with pointy daggers (honey locust, cactus plants).

Get ready! Soap bubbles OR balloons
Magnifying glass

Get set! Find a prickly plant or tree. (A walk through an overgrown field will usually yield numerous "porcupine plants.") Examples: thistle, honey or black locust, cactus plants, yuccas, nettle, teasels, raspberry bushes.

Go!

1. Get as close to the thorns or spines as you can without catching your clothes on them. Very slowly and carefully, place your fingertip on a pointy spine to feel its sharpness.

2. Notice if there are any bugs crawling on the plant or any signs that the plant has been nibbled by bugs, birds or other animals.

3. Blow a soap bubble, or rub a balloon, against the spiny plant and notice if the bubble or balloon sticks to the plant or pops.

(NOTE: Soap bubbles are better for young children who might become frightened by a loud balloon pop.)

Let's talk

Why do some plants have sharp points?

What do the points look like? *(Hint: needles, tacks, swords.)*

Would you like to eat a plant like this?

Would animals like to eat a plant like this?

What would happen if you tried to pull it out of the ground?

Did you see any bugs on your plant? If you did, why weren't they hurt by the spines?

Do animals have prickles? *(Hint: hedgehogs or porcupines, stinging bees.)*

What are some other ways plants can protect themselves from people and animals?

Rooty-Toot-Toot

Learn the importance of two different root systems to the life of plants

The Inside Scoop: The life of a plant depends on how well its root system absorbs water and minerals, conducts them to aerial plant parts, anchors the plant, and stores food. In a **taproot** system, the primary root increases in diameter and grows downward. Younger branchings, called lateral roots, emerge sideways along its length. A carrot has a taproot system; so does a pine tree. In a **fibrous** root system, numerous roots from many locations on the plant, and their branchings, are all somewhat alike in length and diameter. They do not usually penetrate the soil as deeply as taproots. Corn and grass have fibrous root systems.

Get ready! 2 tall, wide-mouthed glass jars (like pickle or mayo)
Garden or other digging tool

Get set! Fill the jars with water. (A drop of food coloring, different for each jar, may be added.)

Go!  1. Find and dig up a dandelion, wild carrot, or other plant with a single long root. Dig down deep around the plant to get as much of its *taproot* as possible.

2. Find and dig up a clump of grass or other leggy, shallow-root plant. Knock off as much dirt as you can from its *fibrous* roots without destroying the branchings.

3. Place each root system in a separate glass. Let the dirt settle to the bottom, until you can clearly see the small branchings.

Let's talk

Which is longer and thicker: taproot or fibrous root?
Which grows deeper?
What would happen to plants if they didn't have roots?
Do roots need water? What might happen to the water in the jars?
What roots can you eat? *(Hint: carrots, beets.)*
What good are fibrous roots? *(Hint: catch surface rainwater.)*
What good is a taproot? *(Hint: deep, solid anchor for plant.)*
Why don't people or animals have roots?
What kind of root system would benefit a small plant growing in dry
    soil? *(Hint: fibrous—to quickly absorb every drop of rainwater.)*

Seed Socks

Learn about one type of seed dispersal

The Inside Scoop: One way seeds are carried from place to place is by hitch-hiking—hooking onto the fur of passing animals. Other means of seed dispersal include: floating through the air and being carried by the wind (like dandelions, milkweeds and maple tree "wings"), or popping out of the parent plant and shooting distances away (like violets and witch hazel). Floating seeds (coconuts) fall to the sand and get swept out to sea, taking root on other beaches. Tumbleweeds roll with the wind, dropping seeds as they go along. When an animal eats fruit, the seeds inside get a free ride and are "planted" when the animal leaves its droppings. The droppings help fertilize the seedling as it grows.

Get ready!   Old pair of big white fuzzy socks (holes are OK)
Magnifying glass

Get set!   Put the socks on over your shoes.

Go!
1. Walk or run through tall grass or a field, particularly one full of seed-bearing plants (like dandelion puffballs).

2. Stop and look at your socks. Name some of the things that are stuck to your socks (seeds, grass, twigs).

3. Keep moving until your socks are covered with seeds and other plant life.

4. Go back to your starting place. Carefully take off your socks. Sort the seeds, grass, twigs, etc., into piles.

Let's talk

How many different groups do you see?

Look at the seed pile. Are there more big seeds or little seeds? What shape are they? Are they prickly or smooth?

Why do seeds stick to your socks?

What happens to the seeds that drop off while you're walking?

How are fuzzy socks like animal fur?

How do animals help carry seeds from place to place?

What other ways can seeds travel?

What can you do with the seeds you've collected?

Why is seed dispersal good for the environment? *(Hint: for variety, plants find new places to grow.)*

Snoring Snapdragons

Observe the nighttime postures of plants

The Inside Scoop: A walk around the flower garden at night would dismay most people. After dark, plants seem to wilt, with sadly drooping leaves and closed flower heads. In a vegetable garden, once hearty-looking plants hang limply, while lettuce leaves stand upright and close together. These are not signs of water shortage but the normal night positions of plants. These movements were first noted in the first century AD by Pliny the Elder, who called them "the sleep of plants." Research has shown that plants, like people, follow a natural rhythm or "biological clock" that regulates cycles of rest and activity.

Get ready! Flashlight

Get set! Make sure the child is familiar with the way a flower or vegetable garden looks during the daytime—flower heads upright and open, leaves open and extended, stems strong and straight.

Go!

1. Using a flashlight, make your way to a familiar garden at night. (Your child may feel less frightened outdoors in the dark if s/he holds a flashlight, too.)

2. Crouching at the edge of the garden, focus your flashlight on one particular section or plant. Then go on to another section or plant. Note the positions of the flower heads, leaves, and stems.

3. Point out plants that seem to have gone to "sleep."

Let's talk

Do plants sleep like people sleep?

How can you tell that the plants are tired?

What will happen when the sun comes up?

Why might flower heads close their petals? *(Hint: to protect their pollen from dew.)*

Do you think anything sleeps inside the closed flower? *(Hint: some insects spend a safe, warm night inside.)*

In what ways are plants and people alike?

If plants and people can't tell if it's day or night, what do you think happens? *(Hint: The rest/activity cycle stays the same.)*

Spiral Sprouts

Observe one way buds and leaves grow on a twig or stem

The Inside Scoop: Spirals are found everywhere in the universe, from giant galaxies to molecules of DNA. On plants and trees, leaves and buds are arranged on stems and twigs in different patterns—*alternate* (placed alternately on opposite sides), *opposite* (directly across from each other), and *spiral* (circling up and around the stem). Leaves arranged in a spiral pattern do not shade each other, assuring each leaf its share of sunshine.

Get ready!

Pruning shears
3-foot length of colored yarn
Coil of wire (from a notebook) or a "Slinky" toy

Get set!

Demonstrate the concept of a spiral design with wire or toy, pointing out the "up and around" growth of the structure. If available, show how vines grow, or talk about decorating a Christmas tree, spiraling lights and garland.

Go!

1. Locate an area with a variety of trees, bushes, and leafy plant life. Study the buds or leaves (or cut samples of twigs) for different patterns:

Opposite - buds/leaves exactly across from each other on the stem

Alternate - buds/leaves placed alternately on opposite sides of the stem

Spiral - buds/leaves circling up and around the stem

2. When you find a spiral pattern, start from the bottom of the stem and wrap the yarn up and around each bud or leaf. This will show you a clear outline of the spiral.

Let's talk

What shape is a spiral—square? round?

Can you find a long blade of grass and wrap it around your finger in a spiral?

How many patterns of leaves did you find?

Why is a spiral pattern good for leaves? *(Hint: they don't shade each other.)*

What else grows in a spiral? *(Hint: shells, vines, galaxies, a tornado, the hair on top of your head.)*

Spore Prints

Learn about one of the identifying characteristics of mushrooms

The Inside Scoop: Each species of mushroom reproduces its own kind by means of tiny **spores** that are dropped from mature plants. Single spores consist of a bit of living matter enclosed within a membrane (like an egg in a shell). They are so small that one spore alone can't be seen without a microscope, but in mass they appear as colored dust. Extremely light, they are carried by wind for long distances. Spore color is one means of identifying a mushroom. Colors range from black, brown, and pink to lilac, green, white, and yellow.

Get ready!
Sheets of white typing paper
Clear plastic cups
Plastic sandwich bags
Basket with handle (an Easter basket works fine)

Get set!
Prepare to look for gilled mushrooms in a moist, shaded area. (Gilled mushrooms look like umbrellas. If you turn the cap upside down, the gills underneath resemble a spoked wheel. Spores form on the gills.)

Go!
1. Place your paper and cups where you can easily return to them, preferably on a picnic table or other flat surface. Then search for mushrooms. When you find one, pluck it whole from the soil, including the stem. (NOTE: Place a sandwich bag over the hand, as a plastic glove, if the young child has a tendency to suck on fingers. Always wash hands after handling mushrooms!)

2. Gather several mushrooms in your basket and take them back to the table. Lay out a sheet of paper. Snap off the mushroom stems and place the caps gill-side down. Cover each with a plastic cup, and top with small rocks.

3. Gather as many varieties as you can find and repeat step 2. Have lunch, play a game, or explore (spore prints take at least an hour). Then uncover your mushrooms.

Let's talk

How many different mushrooms did you find?
What color is the print from each mushroom?
What happens if spore dust blows off the paper?
What are other ways to identify edible mushrooms and their poisonous cousins? *(Hint: by form, color and size of cap, gills, and stem.)*

GUIDED IMAGERY
Growing Toward the Sun

Experience the sensations of growth in a field of sunflowers.

To the narrator: Have the children lie on their backs on the ground. If you are in a quiet place, encourage them to listen to the birds or other sounds of nature. Then read, slowly and with feeling. Perhaps have a snack of unroasted, unshelled sunflower seeds ready.

Let's get comfortable . . . close your eyes . . . and try to see and feel my words. Are you ready?

Imagine you're in a vast farmer's field, lying atop moist dark soil . . . feel the sun warm your face and chest . . . in your mind, scoop up some earth in your hands and squeeze it . . . do you feel small stones and twigs? They help keep the soil porous so rain can soak down to the roots of plants.

You feel so drowsy, so sleepy, lying here under the sun . . . but suddenly there's a tiny tickle right in the middle of your back . . . before you can scratch it, the tickle spreads up around your ears and down to your toes . . . curly green tendrils wrap delicate fingers around you . . . enormous leaves sprout over your head. . . and you feel as though you're on an elevator going UP. Up, up you grow on your leafy bed, toward the sun . . . higher and higher . . . weaving and bobbing on a thick stem . . . hot yellow petals explode in a ring around you . . . you're riding on the face of a sunflower!

Did you remember your hat and sunglasses? Your flower is a real sun-lover . . . all day long its black-and-yellow face follows the sun across the sky . . . from sunrise to sunset . . . east to west . . . every day of its life . . . and across the field, hundreds of sunflowers are doing the same . . . their upturned faces basking in the sun's warmth and light so they might grow bigger, taller, stronger.

People drive by and point, stopping by the side of the road to take pictures of such a glorious curiosity . . . fields of flowers all standing at attention, never letting the sun out of their sight.

But what's going on here? What's all this fluttering and flapping? The flower faces all around you disappear in a flurry of feathers . . . black, brown, and red birds swoop across the field . . . feel the rush of wind as their wings flutter and fan the air over your head . . . they perch on the black spiraled centers . . . like you, riding the sunflowers . . . pecking and shelling . . . and scolding you for sitting on their favorite food—sunflower seeds. Would you care to try some, too?

Play Lightly...

Among the Trees

Tree Hotel

Welcome to the Tree Hotel!
No need for reservations,
Our parking's free —
There's no TV —
But clean accommodations.

May we interest you in:

A twiggy nest to lay your eggs?
A smooth fat limb to stretch your legs?
A big dark hole to rest your eyes?
A mile of trunk for exercise?
A leafy roof to shade your head?
A patch of moss—a king-sized bed?
A feast of pine cones, nuts and seeds?
(Our kitchen serves your every need!)
A secret tunnel deep inside?
A hollow, cranny, place to hide?
A hive for bees? A roost for bats?
A trail for ants? A post for cats?
A place for earthworms down below?
(We'll shelter you from sun and snow.)

Come chipmunks, beetles, snakes and
shrews,
We've got the finest rooms for you.

Come robins, spiders, squirrels and owls,
Just bring your toothbrush, robe and towels.

Welcome to the Tree Hotel!
We're just a humble Inn,
Please be our guest
And safely rest —

May we check you in?

Name Game

Find out how species identification gives a deeper understanding of the natural world

The Inside Scoop: Although common trees are beautiful without names, humans have a need to sort, classify, and name. The formation of distinctions and categories is the first step in ordering the world. Since all things in nature are both related and unrelated—different in some ways and similar in others—the whole process of comparison depends on the notion of categories. To the broad view, a tree is a tree. However, upon closer inspection, each tree has a personality all its own.

Get ready!   Booklet of 3" x 5" or 4" x 6" index cards
2"-wide transparent mailing tape
Pen or pencil
Field guide to trees (not needed until *after* walk)

Get set!   Plan a walk through an area with a variety of trees in leaf.

Go!

1. As you approach each tree, look for signs of life: squirrels, birds, ants, beetles, caterpillars; holes, crevices, nests; piles of acorns, pine cones, catkins, fruit.

2. Pick one leaf from the tree, or find one on the ground, and place it on your first index card. (You can separate the cards from the booklet or leave it intact.) Cover the leaf with a strip of clear tape. If you find signs of fruit—seeds, nuts, catkins, cones—tape them to the back of your card.

3. Write down the location of the tree on each card.

4. Move on to a different tree. Then take all your cards home and match them to the pictures in a field guide of trees. Write the name on each card.

Let's talk

Are all trees the same or different?

Why do people give trees names? What would happen if *you* didn't have a name?

How does a name help you to enjoy the trees in your neighborhood?

If every tree was called "tree," how could you describe the different trees in your neighborhood?

Snag Hotel

Discover the value of dead trees as a habitat for wildlife

The Inside Scoop: Snags, or dead standing trees, are homes to plants, animals and insects that may be different from those living on healthy trees. Diseased and dead trees are more likely to have cavities, or holes, used for nesting sites. Fungi, bark beetles, woodpeckers, bees, squirrels, raccoons and bats find shelter or food on snags. Trees die for many reasons: natural causes like old age, storm damage, and insect infestation, as well as acid rain, car exhaust, and industrial pollution which weaken trees, making them susceptible to insect damage or diseases such as rust, scale, rot and canker.

Get ready!
Magnifying glass and/or binoculars
Screwdriver or prying tool

Get set!
Find a snag to explore, but be cautious. Never climb a snag—dead limbs could easily snap. Don't explore on a windy day when branches might fall.

Go!

1. Look for cavities (holes) where animals might live (but don't disturb them). Be sure to check around the base of the tree as well as the upper trunk.

2. Carefully peel back bark to look for beetles and other insects. Find their holes and tunnels.

3. Look for moss and fungi growing on the snag.

4. Look for evidence of what might have killed the tree.

Let's talk   Name the wildlife that might live in snag holes.
Why is a snag a good place to live?
Why is a snag a bad place to live?
Does the snag have leaves? If not, why not?
Is the wood hard or soft? Rotting or smooth?
How is the bark on a snag different from a healthy tree?
What kinds of insects live under the bark? What are they doing?
Why might snags be dangerous to people?
What might have killed this tree? *(Hint: acid rain, car exhaust, insects, disease, old age.)*

Tree Talk

Learn about a tree by inspecting a cross-section of its trunk

---

The Inside Scoop: A cross-section of a tree has a story to tell. Narrow rings indicate bad growing conditions such as drought, freezing temperatures, or insect damage. Uneven rings reveal unusual growing patterns: leaning against another tree, growing on a slope, or shaded on one side. The age of a tree can be determined by counting its rings, allowing one ring for each year. When a tree is cut lengthwise into boards (instead of crosswise as when it is cut down), the rings are seen as elongated lines (as in furniture). Knots show where a branch was growing out of the trunk.

Get ready!   Measuring tape

Get set!   Point out tree growth rings on pieces of wood furniture, baseball bats, or wooden handles of tools.

Go!

1. Find a stump from a tree that has been cut down and point to the place where the tree started as a baby tree (seedling). Measure the distance from this starting point to the outside on four sides.

2. Count the rings to determine the age of the tree when it was cut down (count one ring for each year).

3. Point to places where the rings are close together or far apart. Look for lines between (perpendicular to) the rings. These are formed by *rays* that store and transport food.

Let's talk

How many years did the tree grow?

Why do you think some rings are closer together than others?

How can you tell if this tree was like other nearby trees? *(Hint: examine the remaining bark.)*

Why do you think this tree was cut down?

If your starting point is off-center, what do you think happened to make it grow that way?

What kinds of things do you use that are made from trees? *(Hint: furniture, paper, wooden toys, fuel, rubber, maple syrup, building materials.)*

Why are trees important? *(Hint: reduce pollution, convert carbon dioxide to oxygen, muffle noise, provide food and shade, reduce soil erosion.)*

GUIDED IMAGERY
In the
Forest

Experience the sensations of a small pine tree in winter.

Narrator: Have the children sit or stand on the ground. Read slowly and with feeling.

Let's get comfortable . . . close your eyes . . . and try to see and feel my words. Are you ready?

Imagine you're standing in a wintry forest . . . hear the wind whisper and *whoosh* through the trees . . . a golden-red sun hangs low in the sky . . . fresh snow drifts around you, sparkling with icy diamond-twinkles on this cold, sunny day . . . see how the smooth whiteness is broken by deer and rabbit tracks, visitors looking for food in this sheltered place.

Somehow, as you stand upright and tall like the nearby trees, you find you cannot move . . . your feet are rooted to the spot . . . down, down goes your taproot, penetrating the earth. Up, up spread your evergreen limbs, reaching for the sky . . . see the leafless tree beside you? It looks frozen and bare after dropping all its leaves last fall . . . but not you . . . you're warm and toasty in your coat of dark green needles . . . when the north wind whips, you bend and sway . . . but your glossy coat never blows away . . .wee animals scurry up your trunk and hide inside your snug coat . . . squirrels and birds flit and hop from branch to branch . . . oooh, that tickles!

But, wait! Someone is coming . . . three figures trudge through the snow . . . oh, no! *People!* What are they doing here? The tall man carries a pack . . . are they coming to cut you down? Will they chop you into firewood? Will they slice you into boards for a table? Will they drag you home and drape tinsel over you?

Squirrels and birds scatter, leaving you all alone . . . a boy and girl run up and point at you . . . the man kneels in the snow, opens his pack, and takes out . . . garlands of popcorn and cranberries! Peanuts and sunflower seeds! They wrap the garlands of food around your body and sprinkle seeds at your feet . . . my, how stunning you look! After the people leave, all your hungry friends—squirrels, blue jays, cardinals, deer and rabbits—come from miles around to enjoy a midwinter feast . . . you are the best-dressed, and most popular, pine tree in the forest.

Play Lightly...

On the Earth

Down Under My Feet

What's going on down under my feet?
Bugs hurry, bugs scurry in the soft green grass —
Leggy spiders, grasshoppers, caterpillar fuzz,
Black beetles, white moths, bees all abuzz.

What's going on down under my feet?
Dig deeper, dig deeper down under the grass.
Bugs tunnel, creatures burrow in the soft dark dirt.
Anthills, worm holes—built without a sound —
Rabbits, moles, and prairie dogs digging underground.

What's going on down under my feet?
Dig deeper, dig deeper down under the grass.
Hard rocks, soft rocks, more rocks than you can count.
Limestone, shale, and granite—big boulders, little stones,
Old fish fossils, and dinosaur bones.

What's going on down under my feet?
Dig deeper, dig deeper down under the grass.
Hot lava cooking from slow melting rock,
Sliding down, pushing up, back and forth it goes,
Exploding ash and fire through the Earth's volcanoes.

What's going on down under my feet?
Dig deeper, dig deeper down under the grass.
A big iron ball lives at the center of the Earth,
Never changed by winter's cold or summer's heat,
Holding all the rocks and dirt and grass under your feet.

Cereal Stones

Observe how surplus groundwater is removed from the soil

The Inside Scoop: Soggy, packed soil is harmful to plant growth. A mix of soil, pebbles and small rocks provides **drainage** so that rainwater can be absorbed into the ground. Water drains more freely into loose ground compared with packed soil. The removal of surplus groundwater by drainage leaves room for air to penetrate the loosened soil, warming it up more rapidly in the spring. This promotes the activity of microorganisms in the soil and improves the soil structure.

Get ready! Empty cereal box with a clear inner bag (make sure it's not stuck to the bottom of the box)
Trowel or small shovel
Container of water

Get set! Find an area outdoors with pebbles or gravel.

Go!

1. Spoon stones into the bag inside the cereal box.

2. When the box is half-full, spoon in some dirt or soil.

3. Spoon in more stones until you've almost reached the top. Add another layer of soil.

4. Carefully remove the inner bag from the box.

5. Slowly pour water over the stones and soil, watching where the water goes.

Let's talk

What happened to the water poured on top?

What happened to the dirt and stones?

Why didn't the water stay on top?

Feel a stone. Is it hard? Or squishy as a sponge?

What would happen if you poured water over a bag full of dirt, with no stones?

Why are stones good for gardens?

Why should there be stones in the soil around your house or apartment building?

Why should there be stones in the soil where garbage is dumped (land-fill)? *(Hint: to prevent odors and insect breeding due to standing water.)*

Drought Garden

Find out how water is conserved using drip irrigation

The Inside Scoop: Water is a valuable and limited resource in many areas. Plants normally need about one inch of water or rain per week, soaking at least eight inches down to the root zone. Many forms of supplemental irrigation—sprinkling, furrows, and hand watering—waste water, since much of it runs off and doesn't reach the root zone. **Drip irrigation** is an ancient, efficient watering system, directing water to the roots in a slow dribble, rather than wetting the entire garden. The controlled moisture content of the soil results in large, quick-growing, disease-free plants.

Get ready!
Trowel and ruler
Plastic milk jug with bottom cut off OR clay pot with drainage hole
Napkin-sized piece of cotton cloth (off an old shirt)
Pail of water

Get set!
Sprinkle water over a garden, or visit your garden after a light rainfall.

Go!

1. Dig down into the garden soil with a trowel, being careful not to disturb plant roots if possible. (To avoid disturbing transplants, do this activity after the soil is prepared but before seedlings are planted.) Feel down into the soil with your fingers, until the moist soil turns to dry soil. Measure the depth.

2. Dig a hole wide and deep enough for your jug or pot. If using a jug, turn it upside down so the neck is in the soil. If using a pot, place it so that the holey bottom is down.

3. Wad up the cloth and stuff it into the drainage hole (it acts as a reverse wick). Pack dirt around the container, *leaving the top open*.

4. Fill the container with water to the top (and keep the container filled during the week).

Let's talk

What happens to the water in your container?
Why do roots need water?
How far down did you dig to find dry soil?
Why is this system better than sprinkling?
How does drip irrigation conserve water during times of drought?
Name some ways people can conserve water in their homes.

Earth Pizza

Learn about the many layers of the Earth's crust

The Inside Scoop: The Earth's crust is the thin outer skin of uneven thickness—thinnest beneath the oceans and thickest where continents exist. We depend on it for fossil fuels, minerals, and vegetation. The outer crust pulses with life, with plants and animals enriching the soil as they live and die. The top layer consists of freshly fallen and partially decomposed leaves, twigs, animal waste, and fungi. The layer under it is a porous mix of partially decomposed organic matter and some minerals. These two layers teem with bacteria, fungi, worms and small insects, and are also home for small burrowing animals. The third layer down is mostly broken-down rock—a mix of sand, silt, clay and gravel.

Get ready!

Old pizza pan
Trowel or sand shovel
Sprinkling can or plastic spray container of water
Scissors or grass clippers

Get set!

Find an area with diggable dirt and an abundance of plant life.

Go!

1. Follow the recipe for an "Earth Pizza":
Sprinkle the pan with small pebbles (rock base).

Dough: Dig soil and pat it over the top of the pebbles. (Return earthworms to their real home so they can continue aerating the soil.)

Sauce: Sprinkle or spray water (rain) over the soil.

Toppings: Add mushrooms, moss, decayed wood, nuts, berries, small pine cones, flower heads.

Cheese: Sprinkle on chopped leaves, twigs, grass.

Bake: In the sunshine!

Let's talk

How is the Earth's crust like a pizza?

What helps plants grow? *(Hint: rain, sun, air, bugs and animals burrowing and dying.)*

Did you find any worms or bugs in your "dough"?

What other animals or bugs live in the soil? *(Hint: moles, beetles, ants, gophers, prairie dogs.)*

What happens to the body of an animal when it dies? *(Hint: consumed by carrion-eaters or decomposes back into soil.)*

Why should people treat the soil carefully?

Sun Trap

Discover how rocks and stones absorb and hold heat and cold

The Inside Scoop: In cities, tall buildings, concrete, and asphalt absorb and store greater quantities of solar radiation than do the vegetation and soil in rural areas. At night the stone-like surfaces in cities slowly release heat absorbed during the day, keeping the air warmer than outlying areas. The term **urban heat island** refers to the fact that temperatures within cities are higher than in rural areas. As well, the huge amounts of heat generated by cars, factories, furnaces, lights, air conditioners, and people cause patterns of air circulation that create a dust dome, trapping pollutants.

Get ready!

2 or 3 fist-sized rocks
Small ice chest

Get set!

Wait for a warm, sunny day. Place the rocks in the ice chest and cover with ice. Carry the ice chest with you when you go outdoors.

Go!

1. Find as many sun traps as you can. Sun traps are objects that hold the sun's heat and feel warm when you touch them. Examples: paved driveways, cars, rocks, bricks, buildings, sidewalks, streets, standing water, benches and curbs . . . and human bodies.

2. Feel the same objects in shaded areas. If they were in the sun at some point during the day, they will still retain warmth.

3. Remove the rocks from the ice chest and feel the cold they have absorbed.

4. Feel tree bark, grass, and other plant life in shaded or sunny areas. Compare to the warmth of sun traps.

Let's talk

Why are things that hold heat called "sun traps"?

Which were warmer: the stone-like objects or plant life? Did you find anything too hot to touch?

What happens to tall buildings when the sun shines on them all day? What happens on cold days?

Why do cities stay warmer than forests?

What happens to the air in cities when heat is trapped?

What are some ways people could help reduce air pollution in cities?

GUIDED IMAGERY
Journey to the
Center of the Earth

Experience the sensations of a flight to the Earth's interior.

Narrator: Have the children sit or lie on the ground. Read slowly and with feeling. If you were to go straight down from where you are to the other side of the planet, do you know where you would come out?

Let's get comfortable . . . close your eyes . . . and try to see and feel my words. Are you ready?

Raise your arms up over your head and clasp your hands together . . . imagine that you're slowly spinning around and around in circles . . . now speed up . . . spinning faster and faster . . . faster than a whirling top . . . suddenly you POP! up into the air and dive back down toward the ground, like a swimmer diving head-first into a pool.

Through the soft green grass you go . . . see who's here beside you—ants and beetles and night-crawlers are busy at work . . . eating and building, enriching and aerating the soil . . . you dive past moles and snakes and prairie dogs sleeping in their tunnels and dark holes and burrows in the soft earth . . . but don't stop here.

Spin faster and dive deeper and deeper, through layers of rock . . . rock so hard only dynamite could crack it . . . rock so delicate that you can flick off layers with your finger-nail . . . big boulders and teeny stones . . . rocks pressed with the skeletons of ferns and ancient fish . . . fossils of life from long before you were born . . . Look! dinosaur bones!

Spin faster . . . dive deeper . . . feel the sweat trickle down your face and taste the salt on your lips . . . whew! It's roasting down here! . . . hot rocks slide back and forth . . . lava gushes up through the rocks and soil, exploding through the Earth's crust, shooting hot molten rock through volcanoes, on land and under the oceans.

Down, down deep you go to the center of the Earth . . . try to spin as fast as you can, for the center of the Earth is a huge iron and nickel ball . . . and you'll never be able to zip through unless you're almost invisible . . . POP! you made it! . . . spinning again through molten rock . . . hard and soft layers of rock, bones, fossils . . . up through the soil . . . say "good-bye" to the woodchucks and voles and worms . . . wave to the ants, grasshoppers, and bees . . . until you spin your way through the grass . . . ending up exactly on the opposite side of the Earth from where you started.

Are you totally dizzy? What a trip!

Play Lightly...

In the Wildlife World

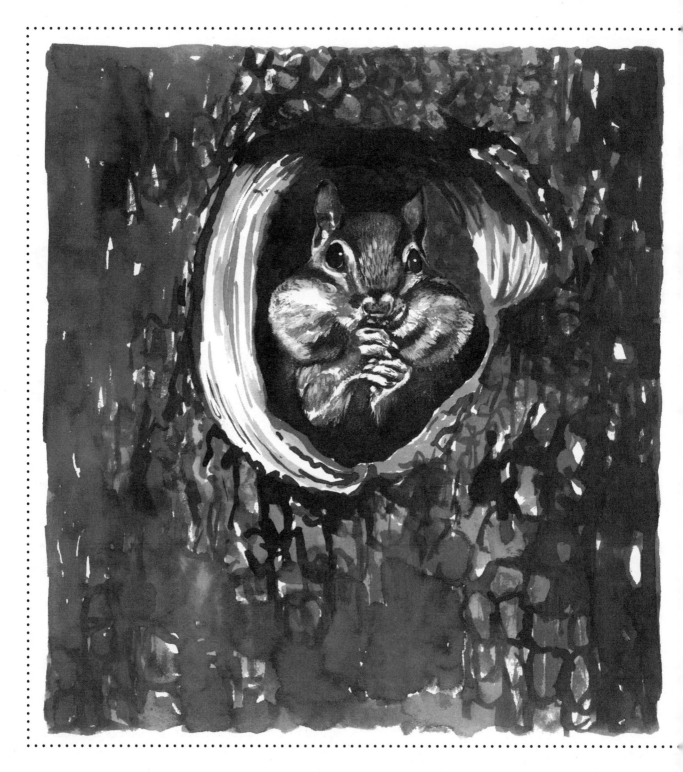

I Spy Animal Eyes

Winking, blinking animal eyes
Watch me while I play outside.

Eyes in bushes, eyes in trees,
Birds' eyes, squirrels' eyes, eyes on bees,
Woodchuck, lizard, owl eyes,
Bulging, hairy eyes on flies.

Lots of animals I can't see,
Hiding, sensing, watching me.

Why this secret peek-a-boo?
Come out, come out—let me see *you!*

Wait! I think I've found a clue . . .
Animal signs, and voices, too:

Fur on bushes, nests in trees,
Feathers, nut shells, rustling leaves,
Pawprints, burrows, piles of poop,
Squeaks, squawks, chirps, a midnight hoot.

Nibbled mushrooms, piles of seeds,
Webs, hives, hollows, trampled weeds,
Dried skins, domes of mud and sticks,
Honks, growls, chatters, whistles, clicks.

When I find an animal clue,
I know you're near—will I see you?

Animal Toons

Compare cartoon animals with their real-life counterparts

> **The Inside Scoop:** Animated domestic and wild animals dominate cartoon shows, comic books, and the Sunday funnies. Anthropomorphism, or giving animals human qualities (e.g., talking, thinking, walking upright, wearing clothes), portrays animals in a friendly but unrealistic fashion, and many children view animals as partly human as a result. On the positive side, cartoon animals encourage interest in, and love for, wildlife. On the negative side, children may believe animals can survive like humans, even if we destroy their natural habitats.

Get ready! Comic or picture books, showing animals with human attributes
Animal cartoon shows

Get set! Point out several favorite animal characters on TV or in movies and books. Talk about how they're like people (talk, walk upright, wear clothes, laugh, live in houses, etc.). Take pictures of cartoon animals outdoors with you.

Go!

1. Name the places outdoors where animals really live—holes in trees, burrows, nests, hives, caves, ponds, bark, leaves, barns and sheds.

2. If a "real-life" animal is available, point out the differences between it and the cartoon character. (This could be done with a domesticated dog, cat, bird or rabbit.)

3. Name places where wildlife couldn't live —shopping malls, apartment buildings, hotels, swimming pools, schools.

Let's talk

How are cartoon animals like people?
Are animals *really* people? How do you know?
Do you like or dislike the cartoon animals?
Do you like or dislike real animals?
Do animals live in houses? *(Hint: some do, but most build nests and other kinds of shelters.)*
In what ways are animals *really* like people? *(Hint: eat and drink, sleep, defecate, work and play.)*
In what ways are animals different from people?
Can animals cry? Laugh? Feel pain? Show love?
If you created a cartoon show with animals, how would you make them act?

Butterflight

Observe butterfly flight patterns and learn how to approach a butterfly at rest

The Inside Scoop: Summer meadows are full of nectar-feeders—bees and butterflies. Butterflies are obvious because of their coloring and characteristic flight patterns (modified depending on whether the butterfly is looking for food, a place to lay eggs, or searching for a mate). Flight patterns may resemble a fluttery up-and-down roller coaster, long low swoops, or a low looping zigzag movement. Instead of trapping and collecting specimens, close-up observation is the least harmful way to study butterflies, as they easily adapt to human presence.

Get ready!   Field guide to butterflies (optional)

Get set!   Locate a meadow full of summer wildflowers OR a yard with a flower garden. (A good butterfly spot is a sunny, flowery place with moisture, woody plants, stumps, banks and walls, and the presence of other animals.)

Go!   1. Walk to a place where you can observe nectar-feeders (do this carefully to avoid disturbing bees).

2. Spot a butterfly in flight and watch its movement:
- Flying in a straight line, but fluttering in an up-and-down roller coaster pattern
- Flying in a straight line, in long low swoops
- Flying in a zigzag, low and looping

3. If you spot a butterfly at rest, *slowly* approach it. (Make sure your shadow doesn't fall across it.) Wipe a little sweat on your finger and place it directly in front of the butterfly. Chances are it will climb onto your finger and drink the salty perspiration. Then try to perch the butterfly on your nose!

Let's talk

What colors are the butterflies you see?
Show me how the butterflies move.
Why does your shadow scare butterflies away?
What are they looking for? *(Hint: food, a place to lay eggs, or a mate.)*
Why do butterflies like flowers? Why do they like your sweat?
How do nectar-feeders help the environment? *(Hint: As they drink the nectar in flowers, a dusting of pollen clings to them which they carry to other flowers. This is called "pollination" or "cross-fertilization".)*

Crepuscular Critters

Observe animals active at dawn and dusk

The Inside Scoop: Many animals are active neither during the day (diurnal) or at night (nocturnal) but are **crepuscular**, or twilight active. Fish, birds, rabbits, deer, voles, mice, and bats are some of the animals active and feeding at dawn and dusk. At dawn, insectivorous birds sing first, followed by the seed-eaters; birds also sing at dusk, though much less noisily. Rodents show two peaks of activity, one at dusk and one at dawn, although they maintain a low level of activity throughout the night. Some day-active or night-active animals will change their habits and become crepuscular—if they are hungry, to avoid competition with other predators, during temperature and seasonal changes, or if they live near humans.

Get ready! Flashlight and binoculars
Clothing in drab colors to blend with surroundings

Get set! Go out at dusk—unless you and your child are early risers—to an area familiar to you (dark comes faster than you think, and it's easy to lose your way back).

Go! 1. Moving as quietly and slowly as possible, find a place to stand or crouch—among trees, near a pond, in a meadow or field, on prairie or desert land, at the seashore, or in a city park. Remember—animals are watching you, too!

2. Shutting out as much human-made sound as possible, listen only to the sounds of crepusculars: birdsong, rustling leaves,

cooing, howling, hooting, squeaking. Try to guess what might be making the sounds.

3. Look for life in silent areas: ponds (feeders close to the surface) or a riverbank (birds waiting for fish or frogs), at the shore at low tide (crustaceans), around city buildings (moths, bats, mice).

Let's talk
Some animals sleep during the day. Some sleep at night. When do you sleep?
What happened first—*seeing* or *hearing* animals?
What are crepuscular animals doing? *(Hint: searching for food.)*
Why is it good for the environment when animals eat at different times? *(Hint: they avoid competition with each other.)*

Don't Bug Me

Discover how insects differ from other bugs

The Inside Scoop: Not all bugs are insects, even though they may look like them. Insects have 3 body parts (head, thorax, abdomen), 6 legs, 2 antennae, and (usually) wings. Spiders, ticks and mites have only 2 body parts, 8 legs, and no antennae. Millipedes and centipedes have numerous body segments and legs. No matter what the designation, bugs are important to humans. Plant species depend on them for pollination, soil aeration, and the decomposition of dead tissue into nutrients. We depend on plants for food, consuming them or plant-eating animals. Without bugs, plant life would disappear, along with humans and wildlife.

Get ready!   Empty, washed baby food jars (or any small glass jars)
White square of cloth (about a square yard of old bedsheet will do fine)
Magnifying glass

Get set!   Poke air holes in the caps of the jars.

Go!

1. Get your jars ready to fill with bugs, with the caps off.

2. Spread your cloth under a bush. Gently beat the bush with a stick. Bugs will fall off onto the white square.

3. Quickly scoop some bugs into your jars or join the corners of your cloth, trapping the bugs inside. Remember, most insects have wings and will try to fly away!

4. Examine your bugs with a magnifying glass. Count the legs. Look for antennae and wings. Then let the bugs go free.

5. Find a spider's web and examine the spider. (Don't capture it.) Count the legs.

Let's talk

Do all bugs have the same number of legs?
Do all bugs have wings?
How do bugs help the Earth? What are some of their jobs? *(Hint: pollination, soil aeration, decomposition.)*
What would happen if all the bugs disappeared?
How do insects differ from other kinds of bugs?
Some bugs eat other bugs. Why do farmers need them?

Locomotion

Observe patterns of animal movement from a different viewing angle

---

The Inside Scoop: Animals that can move—run, leap, slither, swim, or fly—have great advantages. They can find food, escape from predators, and locate new homes. Land animals push against the firm ground, using their limbs and muscles to move across, or burrow into, the earth. Although humans can easily point out moving limbs, animals such as caterpillars, snails, pillbugs, and beetles hide their "moving equipment" underneath their bodies.

Get ready!

Small pane of framed window glass, at least 12" x 24", or larger (please don't use unframed glass as the edges are too sharp and fragile) OR a clear sheet of Plexiglas or Lucite
Plastic cup

Get set!

Decide what you will use to prop the glass, at both ends, up off the ground (at least 1-foot, or high enough for a child to slide head under). Rocks from outdoors will do, or find your own wooden blocks or sawhorses.

Go!

1. Set up your glass "table", making sure there is enough room to slide your head underneath as you lie on your back. When you look up, you should be able to see the sky—but not the sun!

2. Using your plastic cup, gently capture a caterpillar, beetle, snail, or other creature that you would like to watch from below. Put it on your glass table, lie down on your back, and slide your head underneath. You'll be able to watch your bug do the "locomotion."

3. Repeat this with other creatures you would like to observe. Then, let them go free.

Let's talk

Did all of your animals have legs? If not, how did they move?
Did any leave a trail? *(Hint: snails and slugs ooze slime.)*
What can you see from the bottom that you can't see from the top?
Why did you let your creatures go free?
What happens to animals that can't run or fly away when danger is near?

No See'Ums

Learn how animals and insects give clues to their existence, even when they can't be seen

The Inside Scoop: Wildlife exists everywhere, leaving signs that say, "Look! I was here!" Loose feathers, old nests, broken eggshells, and white droppings are a sure sign that birds are nearby. Ants build hills; insects glue their egg cases underneath leaves and twigs. Squirrels leave piles of nuts and pine cones on rocks and tree stumps. Animals leave tracks, scat (droppings), and clumps of fur. Listen for chipmunks scampering through dried leaves; woodpeckers tapping; owls hooting. Any number of wildlife signs can be detected using your sense of sight and hearing.

Get ready!

Basket or pail for collecting clues
Flashlight
Magnifying glass

Get set!

Mark off an area to explore, in a vacant lot, park, meadow or forest.

Go!

1. Look for signs of wildlife: webs, holes and burrows, feathers, nests, hives, fur clinging to shrubs and undergrowth, tracks in the snow or mud, droppings, cocoons, dried skins, scratchings and bits of bark at the base of trees, chewed stumps, domes of mud and sticks.

2. Listen for sounds of wildlife: birdsong, rustling leaves, chirps, squawks, chattering, cawing, buzzing, hooting.

3. Search for signs of eating: empty nut and seed shells, bones, nibbled edges of flowers and leaves, remains of a recent kill, nibbled mushrooms and pine cones.

Let's talk

What clues did wildlife leave behind?
Can you guess who left each clue?
Where have they gone? Why are they hiding?
Did you spot the animals or bugs making sounds?
How do animals sense that people are nearby?
Why do most animals stay away from people?
What are some clues *people* leave behind? *(Hint: litter, footprints.)*
Which sense did you use most—sight? smell? touch? hearing?
    taste? Which sense did you use the least?

Oh, Nuts!

Learn how food recovery patterns prove that animals retain information about their territories

The Inside Scoop: Animals that store food, like squirrels, provide evidence of spatial memory. They have the incredible ability to recover hundreds of pine nuts, acorns, or other food. Chickadees, jays, titmice, crows, and nuthatches hide and recover food within their home territories or up to several miles away. The remembered location of stored food may be brief (less than a day) or recalled over several months, as when acorns buried in the fall are retrieved during the following winter.

Get ready!

10 - 25 walnuts or unsalted peanuts (in the shell)
Equal number of small, colorful markers: golf tees, buttons, key tags

Get set!

Go to a natural area with abundant hiding places for your nut treasures

Go!

1. Think like a squirrel—hide or bury your nut in a place where it can't be seen. If you bury your nut, place a marker on top of the soil. To hide a nut above ground, place your nut on top of the marker. Don't forget to count each one. You're marking your place just in case a *real* squirrel steals your nuts! (NOTE: An older child or adult may want to sketch a rough map showing the approximate locations of the hidden nuts.)

2. Take a break. This is a good time for a lunch break, play time, or a nap for younger kids. Older kids may want to come back a day—or week—later.

3. Without using your map, try to find all of your hidden nuts and/or markers. Use your map only if you're stumped.

Let's talk

Where are some places squirrels might hide nuts?

Did you find all of your nuts? If you didn't, what do you suppose happened?

Did you find any markers without nuts? If you did, what happened to the nuts? *(Hint: stolen by squirrels or peanut-loving bluejays.)*

If squirrels can find their buried nuts months later, what does it mean? *(Hint: they have memory, or "space sense", about their territories.)*

Shadow Play

See how animals protect themselves by concealing their shadows

The Inside Scoop: No matter how perfectly an animal or insect camouflages itself—blends into the background—it will still be seen if its shape casts a shadow. The animals most easily detectable are those living on flat, open ground. They often crouch, or flatten themselves, to blur their outline and minimize the size of their shadow. Shadows can also be made smaller by orientation to the sun—butterflies which close their wings above their back tend to alight facing the sun so that their shadow is reduced to a thin line, or tilt themselves flat. Some marine animals, like rays, flatten themselves and cover the edges of their bodies with mud or sand.

Get ready!

Long-sleeved, adult-sized shirt or sweatshirt which will be over-sized on a child's body (providing "wings" when child lifts arms)

Get set!

Go out on a sunny day, to an area where your shadow has clear definition (a paved, tree-less area works well).

Go!

1. Find your shadow. Use your hands to make tall "ears" on your head (or use branched twigs for antlers, broad leaves, etc.) Name the kind of animal or insect you are. Then turn your body so that your "ears" disappear.

2. Stand up straight and stretch your arms out into "wings", making the biggest shadow you can. Watch your shadow and find a way to make your shadow small.

3. Without hiding behind anything, find a way to make no shadow at all.

Let's talk

Is your shadow bigger or smaller than you are?

Do you have a shadow on a sunny or cloudy day?

How did you make your shadow grow bigger?

How did you make your shadow grow smaller?

How did you make your shadow disappear? *(Hint: lie flat on the ground.)*

If you were a butterfly, how could you make your wing-shadow smaller? *(Hint: fold wings over back and turn to face the sun.)*

Which is easier to spot—an animal with a shadow or an animal without a shadow?

Why do animals and insects want their shadows to disappear?

Snake Slithers

See how movement is possible without arms, legs, or wings

The Inside Scoop: Snakes once had legs—pythons and boas still have internal relics of hip bones. Without legs, snakes have developed a new means of traveling, flexing flank muscles in alternate bands so that the body is drawn up into S-shaped curves, pressing flanks against stones or plant stems and pushing forward. On a completely smooth surface, most snakes simply writhe helplessly. Several species of snakes living in sandy deserts have developed a variation of this technique called **side-winding**. The snake's body takes an S-shape but touches the ground at only two points, leaving a series of sideways bar-like tracks in the sand.

Get ready!   Old sweatshirt or T-shirt
Old pants

Get set!   Pull your arms inside your shirt and clasp your hands behind your back.

Go!      1. Lying on the ground, pretend you're a snake and try to move forward. No feet allowed to help push! (Most kids will lie on their bellies and make side-to-side movements.)

2. Try flexing your muscles like snakes do. Raise your head and pull your shoulders up and forward, then down, and drag the hips forward (in an undulating motion), pushing against the ground.

3. Try a side-winder motion. Lying on your side and keeping the head raised, slide your shoulders forward, then hips and legs. Keep moving forward, at a sideways angle.

Let's talk

Do snakes have arms? Legs? Wings?

Which snake-walk was easier?

Snakes use their muscles to move. Is there a way you can move *without* using your muscles? *(Hint: roll over and over down a hill.)*

Why do you think snakes lost their legs?

Can snakes eat without arms, legs and wings?

How do they catch their food?

Name some of the ways animals move.

Why do you think many people are afraid of snakes?

Name some other creatures without arms, legs, or wings. *(Hint: worms.)*

The Unhuggables

Learn how every insect and animal has a purpose in the natural world

---

The Inside Scoop: Some animals and insects aren't easy to love. They sting, bite, and burrow. They creep, crawl, and slither. They may be physically repulsive to many people, or carry diseases. The first impulse is to destroy such creatures. But each has a job in our natural world—providing insect or rodent control, soil aeration, decomposition, or as food for other insects and animals. Bats eat hundreds of insects every night. Snakes keep rodents from taking over. Worms aerate the soil. Bees pollinate flowers. Species should not be destroyed because they're "ugly."

Get ready! Magnifying glass and/or binoculars

Get set! Name, or find pictures of, animals and insects that are cute (bunnies, chicks, lambs, hamsters, kittens, puppies, lady bugs, caterpillars, butterflies).

Name, or find pictures of, animals and insects that are "unhuggable" (bees, bats, spiders, frogs, beetles, worms, cockroaches, mosquitoes, snakes).

Go! 1. Explore outdoors, but try not to disturb the creatures you're watching. Inspect trees and grass, flowers, shrubs, soil, and puddles. Search under rotting wood, leaves, and rocks. Check the cracks in sidewalks, the corners of old buildings, trash cans. Notice any flying insects buzzing around you.

2. Point out the insects and animals you think are "unhuggable."

Let's talk

What makes some bugs and animals cute?

What makes them "unhuggable"?

Why are many people afraid of unhuggables?

What are the unhuggables doing while you're watching them?
(Hint: flying, jumping, creeping, crawling, running, resting.)

Do unhuggables work? What kind of work might they do?

If they're not biting or stinging you, why should you leave
unhuggables alone?

How do unhuggables fit into our natural world? *(Hint: provide
insect or rodent control, soil aeration, decomposition, provide food
for other insects and animals.)*

Who Am I?

Learn how outdoor explorers use identifying hand-and-body motions to avoid frightening wildlife

The Inside Scoop: Most animals frighten easily at the approach of a human. Outdoor explorers seeking to spot wildlife should walk quietly, keeping their voices to whispers. Even then, wildlife senses human presence. But how can one quietly point out an exciting find? Yelling, "Hey! Look at that!", makes an animal disappear from sight. Outdoor explorers often use hand-and-body motions, as in pantomime or charades, to silently identify wildlife. For example, fingers spread above the head to mimic deer antlers, flapping the arms for bird wings, or clawing motions for bear.

Get ready!   (No materials needed)

Get set!

Name some animals and *silently* act out their identifying traits with parts of your body: hands, fingers, teeth, facial features, etc.
Examples: Clasped arms for elephant trunk
Spread-out fingers for deer antlers
Flapping arms for bird wings
Scratching and swinging for monkey
Tongue-flicking for frog
Finger-clawing and bared teeth for bear

Go!

1. Go to an outdoor area, or walk a trail, where you might see a variety of animals (these may be as common as squirrels, pigeons, toads, worms, ants, grasshoppers, songbirds, spiders, butterflies, etc.).

2. Stand still and carefully look around you.When you spot an animal or insect, point to it or point in the direction you see it. *Without speaking,* use your hands and body movements to identify the animal or insect. (You may flutter your fingers, make soft buzzing or humming sounds, or make gentle hopping or burrowing motions.)

3. If no one else spots your animal, or if it has flown or run away, you may *whisper* it to others (so that other wildlife won't be frightened).

Let's talk

Why did you whisper instead of shout?

Why are some animals afraid of humans?

Can animals and bugs still see you, even if you don't make any noise?

What other ways can animals sense your presence?

Do you think noise from traffic, factories, construction, and airports disturbs wildlife?

GUIDED IMAGERY
Hiding From the Storm

Experience the sensations of a small animal during a thunderstorm.

Narrator: Have the children sit or lie on the ground. Read slowly, dramatically.

Let's get comfortable . . . close your eyes. . . and try to see and feel my words. Are you ready?

Imagine yourself outdoors on a warm summer's night . . . crickets are singing . . . an owl *who-who-whoos* nearby . . . fireflies dance and flicker around your head . . . trees cast ghostly shadows on the ground, under the full moon.

Lift your nose and sniff the fragrant odors floating in the night air . . . what do you smell? Pine trees? Damp earth? Wet leaves and rotting wood? What else? Perhaps the faint scent of a strange animal . . . and a passing human.

Far off in the distance, the black sky is broken with flashes of lightning . . . a slow rumble of thunder shakes the ground under your feet . . . a cloud passes in front of the moon, darkening the forest around you . . . a cool breeze lifts the hair at your neck . . . something is coming . . . what is it?

You look up, and a raindrop hits your nose and dribbles into your mouth . . . then two drops, then three . . . suddenly the sky opens and hard cold rains pelts your head and body . . . lightning strikes closer, lighting up the whole sky. . . the air smells burnt, of electricity and fire. . . a loud BOOM! of thunder makes you leap into the air . . . you've never been so scared . . . Quick! Find shelter, a place to hide from the storm. . . you scamper across the wet grass as fast as you can, searching for your hole in the earth . . . lightning crackles around you . . . and a huge tree crashes to the ground.

Finally you see it—your warm, safe hole . . . layered with soft dry grass and protected by the thick trunk of a tree . . . HOME at last . . . you wriggle down inside, turn in a circle, and lay down on the comfortable nest. Water trickles down your back, but you feel so very safe now . . . outside, the rain falls steadily . . . but gradually the thunder sounds farther away . . . and finally, the storm is over.

Play Lightly...

Among the the Birds

An Un-Scary Scarecrow

I stand in the corn,
Checkered shirt, jeans of blue,
But I never scare birds
Because here's what they do:

Swoop over my head
Pluck straw from my back
Build nests in my pockets
Eat corn for a snack
Line-dance on my arms
Scratch seeds from the dirt
Peck bugs off my pantlegs
Unravel my shirt
Snooze on my shoulders
Fly off with my hat
Perch over my eyebrows
And squash my head flat
Chirp tunes in my ears
Poke beaks up my nose
Leave soupy white speckles
Surrounding my toes
Bring wee fluffy chicks
From every bird nation
Invite feathered friends for
A bird celebration!

No, I can't be a scarecrow
The job is absurd,
It's not that I'm lazy —
I simply love birds.

Egg Toss

Discover how nesting material absorbs shock and affords protection for animals

The Inside Scoop: Anyone jumping into a leaf pile or enjoying a hayride has experienced the cushioning effect of plant life. Many animals (even dinosaurs!) actively build or dig some kind of shelter or nest, weaving and layering soft, strong natural materials—leaves, twigs, moss, grass—into a form which provides a place for rest, hibernation, or the protection of young.

Get ready!   2 raw eggs, in the shell
String, masking tape, yarn

Get set!   Find natural nesting material outdoors—weeds, leaves, brush, thatch, grass clippings, twigs.

Go!

1. Build a protective covering around one egg by layering material around it, holding the layers in place with string, yarn or tape. Keep layering and wrapping until you have a soft, strong ball around the egg.

2. Gently toss the egg-ball back and forth (between child and adult). It's OK if the ball hits the ground. After a while, unwrap your egg enough to see if the egg is still whole.

3. If your first egg is broken, wrap the second egg with different materials. Try dropping your ball from a distance—from a tree or window.

Let's talk

Why are you unlikely to get hurt if you fall into a pile of leaves or tall grass?

Why do animals use leaves and grass to build their nests?

What soft things do you have in your bed?

Why are you wrapping an egg instead of an apple?

Leaves, grass, and moss are soft, but are they strong, too?

Why would birds want to lay their eggs in nests?

If your egg broke, what do you think caused it to break? *(Hint: defective egg, too little protective material, too high a drop, too strong a throw.)*

If you had to build a nest for yourself, what materials would you choose?

Frosty the Birdman

See how winter birds are attracted to a variety of seeds, high-fat foods, fruits, and berries

The Inside Scoop: Not all birds fly south for the winter. For survival, they are constantly on the lookout for food sources in their snow-covered territories. Insect-eating birds such as woodpeckers, chickadees and nuthatches love high-energy suet during cold months. Black oil sunflower seeds have more energy than other sunflower seeds and are a favorite of chickadees, blue jays, and cardinals. Cedar waxwings, cardinals and blue jays are also great fruit and berry eaters.

Get ready!

Wild birdseed mix (sunflower seeds, millet, cracked corn, and other seeds)
Unsalted peanuts in the shell
Raisins, berries, chopped apple and banana
Cereal
Cheese cubes, suet (beef fat), or peanut butter

Get set!

Build a snowman (or snowwoman).

Go!

1. Make a face on your snowperson, using raisins for eyes, a peanut for a nose, and cheese cubes for teeth (or any decorations you like).

2. Don't forget to add fruit, nuts or cereal for buttons, ears or other features.

3. If your snowperson has arms, sprinkle birdseed on them or hang suet from twig arms. Cover the top of the head with seed (or make a "hat" with a board or plate covered with seeds and fruit).

4. Hide where birds can't see you (you may have to watch from a window).

Let's talk

How many birds came to eat? Did they come in flocks or alone?
Were they big or little? What colors?
What kinds of food do birds AND people eat?
Were the birds friendly or did they fight?
How do birds take peanuts out of the shells?
Did you see other animals eating the food? *(Hint: dogs, cats, squirrels, raccoons, mice.)*
Why should you feed birds in the winter?
What kind of feeder would be stronger than a snowperson? How would you make it?

Home Improvement

Learn how birds actively build shelter to keep their young safe from predators and bad weather conditions

The Inside Scoop: When birds are building their nests in the spring, they fly around looking for nesting materials. A nest usually has a framework of twigs lined with softer materials such as fur and hair, moss, leaves, grass, bits of string. Some birds pluck their own feathers to make a fluffy lining. Humans can help birds build their homes by providing a place for "one-stop shopping."

Get ready!   Small woven basket with a handle OR net bag (the kind onions are sold in)
Scissors and ruler
Small pieces of yarn, string, fabric snips, dryer lint (*Do not* use sewing thread or fishing line)

Get set!   Cut the yarn or string into pieces no longer than 4 inches.

Go!

1. Search for more nesting materials outdoors: feathers, unraveled burlap, kite string, old shoelaces, dried grass, small twigs. Cut these to 4 inches or less.

2. Stuff the nesting materials inside your basket or bag. Let some pieces of yarn and string dangle outside.

3. Hang your basket or bag securely on a tree limb, post, fence, or outdoor plant hook, in plain sight for nest-building birds.

4. Watch for birds to pick up the dangling strings and fly away with them.

Let's talk

What kinds of materials do birds use to build nests?

What do people use to build their homes?

Why do birds like yarn and string? Why do they like short pieces? What might happen with longer pieces? *(Hint: catch on tree limbs as bird is flying.)*

If you tracked a bird back to its nest, why do you think it built in that spot?

What's wrong with using sewing thread or fishing line? *(Hint: birds become tangled and can't fly.)*

Why should you be careful about throwing away plastic 6-pack rings? *(Hint: larger birds strangle when their heads catch in the holes.)*

Spishing

See how some species of wild birds easily adjust to human presence

The Inside Scoop: When bird-watchers repeat the words *spish-pish-pish* until they run out of breath, they're **spishing**—and drawing songbirds closer to their area. Far-off chickadees and warblers will sometimes flutter up and surprise a spishing birder. Hand feeding, or hand taming, wild birds is surprisingly easy if you try it with chickadees, titmice, nuthatches, or other small, friendly birds who easily adjust to human presence.

Get ready!   A small plate or container of sunflower seeds

Get set!   Find a location near a bird feeder or where chickadees, titmice, or nuthatches are flitting (birds are more likely to come on a winter day when food is scarce).

Go!   1. Stand very still, holding out your container of seeds.

2. Make the spishing sound with your lips, forcing the "sh" between your teeth *spish-pish-pish* quickly (you might want to practice at home first).

3. If a bird flutters up to eat the seed, don't try to grab or pet it. You'll scare it away. You can talk to the bird, but stay very still.

4. If the birds seem very friendly, you can try putting seed on your outstretched bare palm or on your hat.

Let's talk

Is spishing a way of talking to birds?
Why do they like the sound? What do you think it means?
How many sunflower seeds did one bird eat?
Why should you stay still? What happens when you move?
Why are some birds friendly to people?
What can people do to show friendliness to birds?
Can people and animals live together without harming each other?

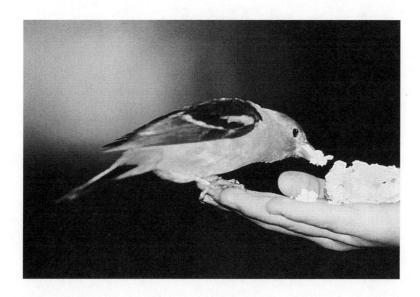

GUIDED IMAGERY
In a
Bird's Nest

Experience the sensations of a fledgling as it prepares to leave the nest.

Narrator: Have the children sit on the ground, perhaps very close together, as if in a nest, in groups of two or three.

Let's get comfortable . . . close your eyes . . . and try to see and feel my words. Are you ready?

Imagine you're sitting in a small round basket . . . pat the soft cushion beneath you . . . it feels as springy as a bed of moss, as silky as the tips of feathers, and as warm and snuggly as milkweed fluff. . . now put your hands up and feel the walls of the basket . . .

so rough and woody, with tiny twigs poking out here and there . . . resting beside you are two smooth brown eggs . . . oh, my . . . this soft twiggy place isn't a basket after all—it's a bird's nest!

Imagine your body covered with wispy chick fluff to protect you from the cold and rain . . . wriggle your long skinny toes, just right for grabbing branches and holding on tight . . . overhead, green leafy branches flutter against a bright blue sky . . . now peek over the side of your nest . . . careful! Don't fall out! The ground is a long way down . . . much too far to jump.

Suddenly a dark shadow covers you . . . someone is perched on the branch above your head, blocking the sun . . . someone big and brown with a pointy beak . . . quick, hide behind the eggs! PLOP! A squiggly, squirmy worm drops on your head . . . mother has brought you breakfast . . . you swallow the delicious worm in one gulp . . . ummm, yummy . . . you try to hop around, jump, and flap your wings, but this nest is much too cramped . . . and you might crack your brother-or-sister eggs before they're ready to hatch.

Mother knows you've grown too big to play inside anymore . . . she gently nudges you to the side of the nest. . . you climb up and perch on the edge with your wobbly clawed toes . . . the ground is still so far away! But you feel brave and much stronger than this morning . . . Are you ready to take a chance? Are you ready to leave your nest and mother? Are you ready to hunt for worms all by yourself? Okay, this is how you do it . . . spread out your brand-new wings . . . catch the wind under your feathers . . . leap up into the air . . . and FLY!

Play Lightly...

In the Human World

A Week at Camp

A week at camp?
No, I won't go!
I'll miss my favorite TV show!

They'll make me eat
Brown nuts and seeds
And sew a necklace
Out of beads.

We'll sing a goofy campfire song
Until a grizzly
Comes along.

They'll make me tote
A two-ton pack
And swat mosquitoes
Off my back.

A week of games I'll never win —
I'm slow and small,
And I can't swim!

A week at camp —
I had a blast!
So much to do,
The days went fast.

I pitched a tent,
I climbed a tree,
And I didn't care about TV.

We told ghost stories by the fire
And watched the moon
Rise higher, higher.

I hoped the week
Would never end,
Because I'd miss
My new best friend.

The games I thought
Too hard to win
Are easy now —
And I can swim!

Backwards Day

Learn how forward-directed eyesight limits observation of the natural world

---

The Inside Scoop: Vision depends on a highly-developed sensitivity to light, with our eyes and brain analyzing position, shape, brightness, distance and movement of objects. The eyes of most insects and crustaceans hold hundreds of lenses, while most fish, birds, and mammals have an adjustable single lens and retina system similar to our own. Humans, apes and monkeys have forward-directed eyes, with an overlapping visual field and depth perception. But for coverage and acuity, human vision takes a back seat to that of birds. With a bird's wide field of view, it can detect movement in all directions—without moving its head.

Get ready!   Plastic sunglasses

Get set!   Talk about the placement of eyes on various insects and animals. Find pictures of animal faces in books, or use domesticated pets as examples.

Go!   1. Walk a path (hiking trail, park, or city sidewalk) with objects to touch: trees, bushes, buildings, playground sets. Name whatever you touch. Then STOP. Announce: "Today is Backwards Day!"

2. Turn your T-shirt, jacket, cap or other articles of clothing so that you're wearing them backwards. Say your name backwards (for example, Whitestone Jessica).

3. Without looking behind you, walk slowly backwards. You can move your eyes from side to side *but not your head.* Name only the things you can see or feel. Put your sunglasses on backwards, so that you have "eyes on the back of your head." Name the things you could see if your eyes were in a different place.

Let's talk

Which way do your eyes point? What about birds? Flies? Squirrels? Rabbits? Fish?

What do animals need eyes for?

Why can't you see out the back of your head?

What would happen if your eyes were on your ears? On top of your head? On your feet?

What's so good about having eyes that can see all around?

Barefoot Hiking

Explore nature through the sense of touch

The Inside Scoop: Skin is not equally sensitive at all points to pressure, temperature, and pain. For example, there are more pressure-sensitive spots at the tip of the tongue and on the fingertips than on the back of the body. On any body, there are usually more pain than pressure spots, and more pressure than temperature spots. The soles of our feet are particularly sensitive after being pampered and protected by shoes. Barefoot hikers claim that this sensitivity enhances their connection with the Earth—they can feel the shapes of pebbles, prickly grass, and warm squishy mud.

Get ready!
A backpack to carry your shoes
Old towel (for wiping dirty feet)
Small first aid kit with tweezers, antiseptic, and bandages

Get set!
Choose a hiking spot free from glass shards. A good "barefoot" place has a combination of grass, pebbles, dirt, mud, and water (in the form of dew, snow, rain or stream), where you can experience *pain* (sharp stones), *pressure* (hard earth), and *temperature* (warm mud puddle, cool grass). Park and nature center trails are great places for barefoot hikes.

Go!
1. Take off your shoes and socks and store them in your backpack (it's better to carry them with you in case bare feet get tired).

2. When walking, step straight down and try not to tip-toe. Say out loud the kinds of sensations you feel: smooth, rough, sharp, prickly, dry, squishy, warm, cool, soft, wet.

3. Point to something you see in nature: a fallen log, moss, dried leaves, etc. Say how you think it will feel. Then test it with your feet.

4. Try to pick up a stick or pebble with your toes.

Let's talk

Do you like to hike barefoot? Why or why not?
Do animals wear shoes? How can they run so fast outdoors?
   (Show pads on the paws of cat or dog.)
Why is it hard to pick something up with your toes?
Why do some hikers walk miles in their bare feet?

Claws, Paws, & Thumbs

See how thumbs aid movement and dexterity

The Inside Scoop: The five fingers, including a thumb, on each human hand are specialized for grasping and clutching, with sensitive pads backed by nails rather than claws. The opposable thumb is not exclusive to primates (human, ape, monkey), but it provides an ability to manipulate all sorts of objects and offers the means for intelligent expression. Many animals have paws, claws or hoofs allowing them the ability to run fast, attack, scratch, and burrow. But they will never be able to type at a computer keyboard or play the piano.

Get ready!   Masking tape

Get set!   Tape your thumb across the palm of one hand. (An older child may want to try this with both hands taped.)

Go!   1. Using only the fingers of your hand, try to pick up sticks and stones, pluck leaves or berries off bushes or trees, and swing from a tree limb or jungle gym.

2. Show the movements an animal can do without a thumb: digging in leaves or dirt, scratching, wiping face and nose, scooping water or sand, feeding from the ground, pouncing.

3. Show the movements a human or monkey can do with a thumb: pick up a bug, grasp a tree limb, draw in the sand, hold on to a swing, tear a leaf in half, peel a banana.

Let's talk

What good is a thumb?

Would you like to have paws or hoofs instead of two thumbs?

Why can't you pick up small objects without a thumb?

Are human hands good for digging holes?

Are human fingers good for clawing and scratching?

What can you do that animals can't do?

What can animals do that you can't do?

Why are thumbs good for writing, painting, sports, and playing a musical instrument?

Forks in the Road

Discover how tools are developed from natural resources

The Inside Scoop: No one knows when utensils were first created, but evidence from archaeological sites shows that knives and spoons were used since humans began hunting. Sharp-edged stones became knives with which to skin animals and cut meat. Curved shells became spoons. Forks, however, are a fairly recent invention. Although fingers provide handy eating instruments, nature supplies a variety of tools for the fastidious.

Get ready!   Blanket to spread on the ground
Paper plate or reusable plastic plate
Assorted foods to cut, scoop, spear and spread: raisins, marshmallows, bread, fruit bits, popcorn, peanut butter, etc.

Get set!   Spread your blanket outside and arrange your food on the plate.

Go!   1. Find your own utensils in nature with which you could eat your food (no fair using your fingers!).

2. Here are some hints:
   Fork - twigs with tine-like branches
   Spoon - curved seashell or nutshell
   Knife - sharp edge of rock
   Spreader - piece of bark or flat rock

Chopsticks - two straight sticks
Kebob spit - sharp stick
Straw - hollow stem

3. Eat your lunch with your nature utensils IF they're clean. Otherwise, go ahead —now you can use your fingers.

Let's talk

What were your utensils made of?
What could you put your food on if you didn't have a plate?
   (Hint: leaves, flat rock.)
How do animals eat?
What did people use before utensils? *(Hint: fingers!)*
Are humans the only tool-users? *(Hint: chimpanzees use sticks to eat bugs.)*
Name some things you use every day, like a comb, toothbrush,
   towel. Could you find a replacement in nature?

Nose Hike

Learn how animals use smell to gather information about their environment

> **The Inside Scoop:** Human noses are not particularly sensitive to smells, so we can't appreciate how much information an animal gets by sniffing its surroundings. Many kinds of insects, fish, and dogs have especially good sniffers. By defecating, urinating, and marking with scent glands, animals maintain their territories and identify one another. They use odors to give alarm, to select food, and to mate. Odors suggest, stimulate associations, evoke, frighten and arouse, but humans seem to lack the exact words to describe odors.

Get ready!

Knit ski hat
Several paper bags to hold "good"-smelling items, like perfume, deodorant, soap, cinnamon, vanilla, popcorn, orange, etc. AND "bad"-smelling items, like cut onion, sour milk, old sneaker, ammonia-soaked cotton, rotten egg, garlic

Get set!

Pull ski cap down over eyes, leaving nose free, and sniff each bag. Tell if "good" or "bad" and guess what each is. Tell how you feel after smelling each: happy, sad, afraid, angry, tired, hungry, etc.

Go!

1. Go outdoors and smell the scents of nature (particularly after a warm rain). Sniff tree bark, pine tree needles, rocks, puddles, flowers, grass, moist soil (and trash!).

2. Tell which odors smell "good" and which smell "bad." Tell how the odors make you feel.

3. Pretend you're an animal. Sniff the air and the ground for any odors.

Let's talk

What would happen if you didn't have a nose?

What kinds of things outdoors smell good?

What has a stinky smell?

How does smell help you eat? *(Hint: flavor comes from sniffing aromas or exhaling them through the nose as you drink or chew food.)*

Did you smell anything in the air? What do you think dogs smell when they sniff the air?

How does smell help animals survive? *(Hint: helps them select their food, mark territories, find their mates, protect themselves from predators.)*

Pack It Out

Find out how people show respect to the Earth on their visits to nature

---

The Inside Scoop: Wilderness areas provide recreation for a growing number of hikers and campers, as well as providing habitats for wild plants and animals in a living laboratory where nature is at work. Unfortunately, nature suffers when visitors neglect to clean up after themselves, leave exposed trash, feed wildlife, start forest fires, and pollute streams. One way to keep human activities from destroying natural areas is to "leave no trace"—making sure we leave the Earth in as good (or better) shape than we found it.

Get ready!
Child's backpack
High energy snacks (raisins, nuts, chocolate)
Container of juice
Sand shovel or trowel
Band-Aids or small first-aid kit
Light sweater or wind breaker
Whistle

Get set!
Fill the pack with the listed items, and find an easy hiking trail

Go!
1. Start out on a hiking trail, walking until the child needs to break for food and drink. Demonstrate how hikers and campers clean up after eating—by "packing out" or carrying their trash with them, in their packs.

2. Show how hikers go to the bathroom—when there isn't one! Far from any stream, dig a hole in the ground, explain its purpose, and show how to cover it up again. (You'll have to be creative with this one.)

3. Talk about why a first-aid kit and whistle are important. Show how three whistles *"tweet-tweet-tweet"* means "I need help!" and should only be used in an emergency.

4. Clean up the area where you ate, making sure you "leave no trace" of your presence.

Let's talk

Did you bring everything you needed on your hike?
Why should you carry your trash with you?
Why isn't it a good idea to feed wild animals?
How does human activity disturb wildlife?

Rock Art

See how early humans used natural pigments to paint figures on rock surfaces

The Inside Scoop: Prehistoric artists left astonishing paintings and engravings on the rock walls of their surroundings. Bulls, deer, horses, bison and human figures tell colorful stories of hunting-magic rituals, long after the disappearance of the painters. The artists favored vivid shades of yellow, red, brown, black and white, made by mixing minerals or plant parts with a liquid, and applied with feathers, animal hair brushes, or other simple implements. The artists preferred to paint on walls that were smooth and of light uniform color. However, sometimes a detail on the rock's surface was incorporated into the motif.

Get ready!

4 or 5 plastic containers (soft-oleo tubs are fine)
Small container of water or vinegar
Watercolor brushes or wooden ice-pop sticks
Towel for wiping stained fingers

Get set!

Find a smooth rock surface, flat or upright at a child's height.

Go!

1. Search for colorful flower petals, wild berries, soil (clay, charcoal, sand), green leaves. (Any juicy, dark fruit like raspberries, strawberries, blackberries, blueberries, cherries, purple grapes, etc., leave vivid stains but may have to be bought if not available outdoors.)

2. Divide your materials into the plastic containers. Mash or crush the contents with a rock or fat stick, adding a little water or vinegar if the mixture is too dry.

3. Using your paints, create a picture on the rock face, either with brushes, wooden sticks, or fingers. (NOTE: These stains are not permanent and will eventually wear away or wash off in rain, unlike prehistoric rock art.)

Let's talk

Is the Earth a colorful place? Which plant makes the best color? Why did you crush your flowers or berries?
Why did people who lived a long time ago mix their own paints?
Why do people like to paint?
Why did people paint cave walls?
Some people spray-paint words on buildings. It's called "graffiti."
    Why is graffiti-painting harmful to the environment?

Say My Way

See how natural forms can be classified by a variety of descriptive names

The Inside Scoop: Spoken language reflects an overall worldview. Native Arctic peoples, for example, use a variety of different names to describe snow. Snow is very important in their lives—sometimes making the difference between life and death, eating and starving—and they must be able to distinguish subtle differences in their environment. Since these differences are unimportant to most of us, our single word "snow" lumps all of our perceptions of this cold white stuff into one category.

Get ready! (No materials needed)

Get set! Find an outdoor area with a ground cover of: snow, sand, gravel, dew, grass, clover, etc. OR go out on a snowy, windy, or rainy day.

Go!

1. Say the name of the precipitation or ground cover, and describe something about it. For example, SNOW is cold, wet, white, but it also can be hard, icy, round (sleet) or soft, pretty, delicate (snowflakes).

2. Using all the senses, touch with hands and taste with the tongue; point out the different forms; listen for blowing, whistling, thunder.

3. Pretend SNOW (or rain or wind, etc.) had no name. Based on its *appearance* and *your sensations,* give snow some names. For example: "Sparkling jewels," "cold bee-stings," "white feathers," "hard water," "soft blanket."

Let's talk

Can things have more than one name?

How did you decide on the words to use for your name?

Why is it important to have lots of names? Why is it important to have one name?

How would you describe snow or rain to someone who had never seen it before?

Using other words, how would you describe your hair? Teeth? Fingernails?

Some people use names like this in their work. Who are they? *(Hint: poets.)*

Trick-or-Trash

Try a creative way to properly dispose of trash for a cleaner environment

The Inside Scoop: Cleaning up the local community is a small step with a big environmental payoff. Although littering is still a national problem, recycling is making the biggest difference in our trash disposal. New packaging laws and bottle bills make it easy for residents and businesses to recycle, but there are still many other ways individuals can help clean up the Earth.

Get ready!
Old Halloween costume and mask
Small plastic sandwich bags

Get set!
Sew the arms and legs of the costume closed, or rubber band them; sew or pin the back, leaving a wide neck opening.

Go!
1. Take a walk through a park, empty lot, or along a road—anywhere people have been littering.

2. Pick up any litter you find and stuff it inside the costume (use the plastic bags as gloves if you find sticky things). Use recyclable cans and bottles to fill out the legs and arms of your costume. Stuff the body with paper trash.

3. Take your "body" back home and cut off the arms and legs to release the recyclable items—then recycle them!

4. If you didn't find any recyclables, top your litter-person with a mask and leave it out for the trash collectors.

Let's talk   What should people do with their trash?
Did you find more cans or bottles? Plastic or paper?
What can you do with the cans and bottles?
What happens to the environment when people throw trash
  anywhere?
Do animals like trash? Why or why not?
How can people reduce the amount of trash they generate?

GUIDED IMAGERY
Floating Downstream

Experience the sensations of a river ride from city to country.

Narrator: Have the children sit or lie on the ground. Read, quickly or slowly, dreamily or sprightly, as the text requires.

Let's get comfortable . . . close your eyes . . . and try to see and feel my words. Are you ready?

Imagine you're sitting on a bright red maple leaf . . . twirling, swirling down, down . . . then lifted by a gust of wind . . . soaring like a glider . . . across the park, high over the swings and baseball diamond. Far below, see the street lamps flicker on . . . while tiny moving specks of cars carry people to stores, work, and back to their apartments in sky-high buildings.

Your leaf slowly drifts down toward the river where a flat barge silently cuts through the water, hauling supplies to the next city . . . you skid across the water, skipping like a flat stone . . . and off you go with the current . . . rocking gently, drifting lazily, while hungry fish surface and nibble at unsuspecting bugs.

Suddenly the air around you feels different . . . damp and misty . . . you hear a rushing noise, then a soft roar . . . your leaf-boat rushes through the water, faster and faster . . . Oh, no! Rapids! Hang on tight! Your fragile leaf trembles and shakes . . . better clutch the sides with your fingers and toes . . . Here it comes—SHOOSH! off you go on a wild roller-coaster ride . . . walls of water spray up over your head . . . swerving and dipping, plunging and crashing through the bubbly froth. Finally the river calms, and you float under an overhang of autumn trees with leaves of red, gold, and purple . . . dropping leaf- boats into the water. Two hikers crouch at the river's edge, splashing cool water over their hot faces. Float on through pasture and farm fields . . . cows raise their heads and stare at you . . . a farmer sits high on his tractor and waves his hat . . . daisies and black-eyed Susans nod and bob as you pass . . . dragonflies dart and hover in mid-air. This river is full of life—human, plant, and animal . . . without clean water, life would disappear from the Earth.

You can stop here if you'd like . . . or stay on board and float farther . . . for days and days . . . through city and country . . . until you finally reach the ocean.

Play Lightly...

In the Sky

...A Meteor

A meteor shower! A meteor shower!
It's raining stars!
A meteor shower!

Forget your umbrella,
This shower is dry,
It's raining, it's pouring,
Hot *stars* from the sky.

Shower

A meteor shower's
A downpour of lights,
A shooting-star party
Of meteorites.

A glowing white tail,
The mark of its flight,
Leaves a streak in the sky,
As it crosses the night.

It's sparkling, bedazzling,
It's razz-a-ma-tazzling,
It's fiery and blazing and bright.
This show is incredible,
Can't-go-to-bed-able,
Glowy and showy white light.

Exciting, delighting,
The party's all-nighting,
It's dreamy and gleamy and clear.
It's movie-marquee-able,
Turn off TV-able,
The snazziest show of the year!

Moon Illusion

Observe the moon's brightness, and how its size is often overestimated and underestimated

The Inside Scoop: Why the full moon appears different sizes at different positions is still not fully understood. The rising moon near the horizon often looks larger than when it is overhead, even though its distance is basically unchanged. Because the full moon is the brightest object in the night sky, we tend to overestimate its size—and, since we typically perceive night as darkness, we tend to underestimate the moon's ability to illuminate our surroundings.

Get ready!

A quarter and a dime
Picture book with text (or a bedtime story book that mentions, or includes an illustration of, the moon)

Get set!

Go outside on a night when the moon is full, as far away from human-made lights as possible.

Go!

1. Cover one eye with one hand. With the other hand, hold the quarter between your fingers and lift it up to cover the moon. Make the moon completely disappear. Do the same thing with the dime. Then try the tip of your pinkie finger or a tiny pebble. Find the smallest object you can to cover the moon.

2. If the full moon is at the horizon, make a circle with your fingers (like a telescope) and look at the moon only, blocking out any scenery. Tell if it looks larger or smaller.

3. Open your book and try to see the pictures. See if you (or an adult) can read by the light of the moon.

Let's talk

Look at the moon in the sky. Look at your dime. Which looks bigger?
Did your dime cover the moon?
What is the smallest object you used to cover the moon?
Is the moon really as small as a dime? *(Hint: when big things are far away, they look small.)*
Can you see your shadow by moonlight?
Can you read by moonlight?
If you were lost on a night with a full moon, would you be able to see your way?

Skyglow

Identify sources of light pollution in city and rural areas

The Inside Scoop: Even if you don't live in a city, you almost certainly can see a city's glow on the horizon. The sources of skyglow are many: streetlights, parking lots, shopping plazas, office buildings and other businesses using signage and spotlights. Light pollution is caused by excessive or misdirected outdoor lighting, costing cities millions of dollars in utilities charges, and interfering with observers' views of the planets and stars in the night sky.

Get ready!   Binoculars and flashlight

Get set!   On a moonless night, find a flat open area where you have a view of the horizon all around you, as far from human-made illumination as possible (in a city, an apartment building rooftop will *surround* you with skyglow).

Go!

1. *If you live in a rural area:* Stand in one spot and slowly turn around in a circle. Point out areas of skyglow near the horizon, where the sky seems bright compared to other parts of the night sky. Use your binoculars to determine what is causing the glow.

2. *If you live in a city:* Locate areas around you that seem to shine brighter than others. Tell what is causing the light: streetlights, signs, buildings, airport, shopping center, etc.

3. If the night is clear, look for stars in the sky. Point to where the stars shine brightest. Then look for stars in the skyglow.

Let's talk

What makes the sky so bright in some places?

If you were in an airplane flying overhead, what could you see looking down?

What are some of the things in your neighborhood that give light at night?

In what part of the sky did stars shine brightest? *(Hint: areas far from skyglow.)*

Why is it hard to see stars in the skyglow area?

What would happen if the Earth was one big city?

What can people do to cut down on skyglow? *(Hint: install directed lighting, shield light sources, turn off lights that aren't needed.)*

Star-Light Stories

Observe how the human mind searches for patterns in the night sky

The Inside Scoop: The constellations are sky pictures with ancient stories behind them. In times past, they were named for heroes, beasts, and gods, and were believed to have an influence upon humans. Once the stars and constellations were named, they were no longer strange. The night ceased to be a lonely place; instead, the dark was populated by old friends who came out every night. The stars of a constellation are not necessarily related, although they may belong to a loose cluster. In most cases, the stars are at vastly different distances from the Earth and vary greatly in size and brightness. They seem to form patterns simply because we see them all in approximately the same direction.

Get Ready!   Flashlight with a strong, thin beam
Blanket for the ground

Get Set!   Wait for a starry night, preferably moonless and far from any source of light.

Go!

1. Spread your blanket on the ground and lay down flat on your back.

2. Let your eyes adjust to the bright stars against the darkness. If you know the names and locations of some of the stars and constellations, like the North Star in the Big Dipper, point them out.

3. Find a pattern of stars that you like. Shine your flashlight up to the sky and "draw" an imaginary picture using the stars.

4. Make up a story about your star creation, or tell one from a fairy tale or bedtime book.

Let's talk

How many bright stars can you count?
Do some parts of the sky have more stars than other parts?
What are some words that describe stars?
Do you think the stars are hot or cold?
Do you think the stars are close or far away?
Which star is close to the Earth? *(Hint: our sun.)*
How many patterns can you find in the sky?
Why do people make up stories about the stars?
If a star is bright, does that mean it's closer to Earth? *(Hint: no, it may be larger or hotter than other stars.)*

GUIDED IMAGERY
Across
the Galaxy

Experience the sensations of a flight to the stars.

Narrator: Have the children lie on their backs. If this guided imagery is conducted during the daytime, perhaps have them put something over their closed eyes to maximize the darkness.

Let's get comfortable . . . close your eyes . . . and try to see and feel my words. Are you ready?

Imagine yourself outdoors on a moonless summer's night, lying on a blanket under the stars. The air is warm and still. Now hold up your hands and wiggle your fingers . . . you can barely see them in the inky darkness . . . a totally black night, perfect for checking out stars . . . *yee-ouch!* Mosquitoes like hot summer nights, too!

Look up, look up . . . the clear black sky is dotted with pinpoints of light . . . if you could lie here all night, the whole pattern of stars would move slowly in a circle with you at the center . . . long ago, people thought the night sky was the dome of heaven, sprinkled with lamps carried by the gods . . . they saw pictures in the stars . . . animals, women and men parading across heaven's dome . . . an awesome movie theater in the sky . . . if you had a super-long pencil, could you connect the star-dots and draw a picture?

Now imagine your body rising from the blanket . . . speeding through space . . . to the nearest star . . . whoa! Slow down! You almost flew right by it—the nearest star is our own Sun . . . hiding at night on the far side of the Earth.

Now off through the galaxy at light-beam speed . . . let's head for a cluster of stars . . . keep your distance . . . don't get too close . . . stars look twinkly and tiny from Earth . . . but they're really colossal fireballs . . . glowing in rainbow colors—red, orange, yellow, green, blue, and white . . . from far away, you can feel the heat . . . hotter than a burning fireplace . . . hotter than the inside of an oven . . . hotter than beach sand on your bare feet . . . masses of gas shoot out flares in a halo of fire . . . see whole stars explode, brightening the sky with the light of a million suns.

As you slowly fall back to Earth . . . heading for your home and your blanket . . . our nearest star is peeking over the tops of the hills . . . warming the land and all living things . . . the stars overhead fade and seem to disappear in the growing light . . . but don't worry, they're still in their places . . . only hidden by the light of the Sun . . . and waiting for tonight's darkness . . . for the best show on Earth.

Play Lightly...

Together
As
One World

Play Lightly on the Earth

Play lightly on the Earth,
Step gently through the trees,
Treat kindly all the wild things
With claws and scales and feathered wings
With silken fur or itchy stings,
Step gently through the trees.

Play lightly on the Earth,
Step gently on the land,
Treat kindly all the sprouting seeds
The tender shoots and marshy reeds
The newborn buds and meadow weeds,
Step gently on the land.

Play lightly on the Earth,
Step gently in the stream,
Treat kindly all the lakes and seas
The coral reefs and island keys
The turtles, whales and manatees,
Step gently in the stream.

Play lightly on the Earth,
Sing softly round the world,
Treat kindly in this living place
All human beings of every race
One people sharing precious space,

Play lightly on the Earth.

Beginnings & Endings

Observe the transitions in nature from birth to death

The Inside Scoop: Everything that is born dies, and there are natural cycles, beginnings and endings, to all things. Objects around us change constantly because they are made of atoms, which can assemble and disassemble. Change is inherent in nature: flowers bloom and die, earthquakes transform the landscape, animals hunt and eat each other. Yet there seems to be a deeper stability underneath this surface chaos. Marigold seeds always grow into marigolds. Spring arrives after winter. The sun rises and sets and rises again. Permanence persists through changes between birth and death.

Get ready! (No materials needed)

Get set!

Talk about things that have a beginning and an ending: story-books, movies, TV shows. Talk about things that change but stay the same (have a cycle of beginnings and endings): seasons, leaves on trees, the moon, day and night, the human body (specifically hair, teeth, fingernails, cells), clouds, grass. Talk about things that are born and die: flowers, vegetables, animals, people (this is a good time to talk about a pet or relative who has passed away).

Go!

1. Look outdoors for plants and animals in stages of beginning and ending. You might find dead insects, hatching birds, flowerbuds, fallen leaves, new grass, a beehive, green tomato or strawberry, compost pile, rotting log, animal remains, treebuds, sprouts. Call it out—"BEGINNING!" or "ENDING!"

2. Point to objects that you think have no beginning or ending. (Children often think rocks, mountains, sky, and trees live forever.)

Let's talk

Was your birth a beginning or ending?
Did you find more beginnings or endings outdoors?
What would happen if everything lived forever?
Tell what happens after you plant a seed.
Why is death good for the environment? *(Hint: controls population, enriches the soil through decomposition, provides food source for animals.)*

Coats of Many Colors

Learn about the colorful diversity of nature and the usefulness of camouflage

---

The Inside Scoop: All life forms are colorful. Color is used as protection and decoration, sometimes as distinctive as zebras or as unnoticeable as a praying mantis. Animals and insects that blend in with their surroundings are camouflaged, making them difficult to see. Camouflage involves colors and patterns, the overall shape of an animal, and its behavior. The mountain hare has a brown summer coat, molting to white fur for camouflage in snow. The patchy brown of deer makes them almost invisible in woodland shade.

Get ready!

Pack of multi-colored construction paper
A selection of paint-chip cards from a paint or hardware store, to match your paper colors

Get set!

Arrange the papers on the ground or atop a picnic table so that you can easily reach each color without stepping on the others (if the day is windy, anchor each piece with a rock).

Go!

1. Carrying your paint-chip cards with you, search the natural surroundings for objects to match your colors. Place each object on the corresponding colored paper.
Examples:

  green - grass
  yellow - dandelion
  red - rose petal
  brown - pine cone
  black - rock

2. Find as many objects as you can for each color. If you use wildflowers for your colors, pick only a few petals—not the whole flower.

Let's talk

What colors are the easiest to find? The hardest?

Is there a color you couldn't find at all?

Could you find some of your colors in the sky? *(Hint: day - blue; clouds - white; night - black; sun - yellow; rainbow - primary colors.)*

What would the world look like without color?

Why do people love flowers?

Can you name an animal for each color?

How could an animal or insect hide from predators? *(Hint: blend in with surroundings; camouflage.)* Name an animal and point to where it might hide.

Home Sweet Home

Notice how living things are dependent on the physical aspects of their environments

---

The Inside Scoop: A shark can't live in the desert; neither can a cactus live at the bottom of the ocean. Living things are dependent on the physical features of their environment—whether it is warm or cold, wet or dry, shaded or bright. Even the slope of the ground or angle of sunlight may be extremely important. An ample food supply and the right physical conditions impose limits on where livings things are found and the number that can be supported. The community and its physical environment is an **ecosystem**, from the Greek word *oikas*, meaning "house."

Get ready!　　(No materials needed)

Get set!　　Ask your child to describe his or her own house. Examples: warm and dry, a safe place to sleep, has lots of food and drink, full of toys and music.

Go!　　Find a plant or animal (bugs, too) outdoors and describe its "house" or physical aspects of its environment. Then tell where it would not be able to survive.

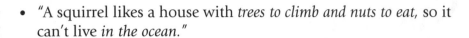

Examples: (child fills in the blanks)
- "A palm tree likes a house that's *warm and sandy,* so it can't live *at the North Pole.*"

- "A squirrel likes a house with *trees to climb and nuts to eat,* so it can't live *in the ocean.*"

- "A worm likes a house with *dirt and grass to tunnel through,* so it can't live *at the top of a tree.*"

- "A fish likes a house with *water and bugs,* so it can't live *in my teacher's car.*"

Let's talk

Is there any place where you couldn't live? Why?

Humans need to eat, drink, and have a safe place to sleep. Do plants and animals need these, too?

How would you feel if someone destroyed your house? Do you think a plant or animal likes having its house destroyed?

Why is it good that living things have to live in different places?

How can humans protect the places where plants and animals live?

Wee World

Inspect the variety of plant and insect life in a microhabitat

---

The Inside Scoop: The world would look different if you were only a few inches tall. Grass would be a jungle; worms as big as pythons. A habitat is an area that supplies food, water, cover, and space. If one of these items is missing, an animal will not use the area for its home. A microhabitat is a very small area that provides these necessities. Because animals require different kinds of food, cover, water, and space, a habitat that is good for one may not be sufficient for another.

Get ready!

Tiny toys, such as miniature cars or action figures
Sheet, with three foot diameter hole cut in center
Shallow bowl of water

Get set!

Find a grassy area and spread out your sheet.
Put the bowl of water in the middle.

Go!

1. Lie down on the sheet, outside of the open circle, with your head close to the ground.

2. Inside the grassy circle, find a safe place for your people to live, sleep, eat, drink and bathe. Take your people for a walk through their world exploring worm holes, ant hills, leaves, clover, flowers. Let them climb over sticks and rocks, and swim in their water.

3. Find some natural objects that might be useful to people in their world:

> Mushroom cap for a pillow
> Piece of bark for a table or surfboard
> Round pebble for a bowling ball
> Acorn cap for a hat
> Leaf for a blanket

Let's talk

Did you find food for your people? A place to sleep?

Why do people need water?

What kinds of animals or bugs live in your world? Did you find their homes?

If you were little, how tall would flowers and grass be to your body?

Did you find any signs of *real* people? *(Hint: litter.)*

What's happening under your feet when you walk through the grass?

How can you show respect to habitats other than your own?

Magic Square

Identify relationships within associations of plant and animal life in a specific environment

---

The Inside Scoop: The natural world is a complex whole. Ecology is the study of living things in relation to their surroundings, or environment, and how each species is influenced by all the other species around it, interacting as a kind of community. A Magic Square is also a whole. The square encloses an arrangement of numbers, so that the totals of each row—horizontal, vertical, diagonal—are all equal (in this case, 15).

Get ready!   Chalk or 8 long sticks of the same length

Get set!   Mark off the lines of a magic square like this:

Draw lines with chalk if you're on a paved area. Arrange sticks if you're on grass. Or draw lines in the sand if you're at the beach or standing on dirt.

Go!   1. Notice the environment around you. Choose a family of interconnected items and count out pieces to fit in your square, placing them in this pattern:

4	9	2
3	5	7
8	1	6

For example:

> **Woods** - you might count out 4 leaves, 3 twigs, 8 acorns, 9 berries, etc. or
>
> **Beach** - 8 shells, 1 driftwood, 3 fishbones, etc.

2. Tell how the pieces are related to each other in the environment you chose.

3. Count the totals—up, down, across, diagonal. The total each way should add to 15 pieces.

Let's talk

How many pieces can you count in a row? Are all rows the same number?

Where did each piece come from? Trees? Soil? Water? Plants?

Why do the all the pieces belong together, even though each box in the square is different?

Name something that would be out-of-place in your square.

(Hint: a cactus plant on the beach.)

My Body is the World

See how the human body mirrors forms found in nature

The Inside Scoop: Nature comes in many shapes, sizes and colors—and humans, as life forms of nature, reflect these variations. Compare, for example, the human body with a tree. A human body has a main torso (trunk), skin (bark), arms (branches), legs (roots), and hair (leaves). Trees, as well as humans, need water, sun, air, and nutrients in order to grow. The differences in color, size, and shape of trees are comparable to the differences found in people around the world.

Get ready!   Masking tape, clothespins, plastic-coated clips, tacks
Old magazines or catalogs
Scissors

Get set!   Cut out pictures of human body parts—legs, arms, heads, fingers, eyes, etc.

Go!

1. Find an area outdoors with an abundance of plant life.

2. Choose a picture and try to find a matching object in nature. Using tape or pins, *carefully* attach your picture to the plant part. Tell why you think they are alike.
Examples:

      Twigs like human fingers
      Grass like human hair
      Tree knots like eyes
      Flower stems like legs

3. After you have used all your pictures, look around at the many ways nature is like you, and you are like nature.

4. Take your pictures with you when you leave the area.

Let's talk
Can you find places for all your pictures?

How is a tree like your body? You have a name. Does a tree have a name, too?

Why should you take your pictures with you when you leave the area?

Plants grow in many colors and sizes. People also come in many colors and sizes. How are plants and people different? *(Hint: plants don't fight or make fun of each other's differences.)*

Picture Me

Recognize the similarities and differences among living and non-living worlds

---

The Inside Scoop: Everything on Earth is interrelated, sharing common origins, adhering to the same physical laws that govern the organization of matter and energy, and having the same molecular basis of inheritance. Although there is unity, there is also diversity in appearance and behavior. We consider birds living; rocks nonliving. However, at a deeper level, birds and rocks are all composed of the same raw materials (protons, electrons, neutrons). The structure and organization of the living and nonliving worlds arise from the same fundamentals, differing only in the degree to which energy is used and materials organized.

Get ready!   7 squares of white paper or large index cards
Marker pens or crayons

Get set!   Go to any outdoor location with a variety of plant and animal life.

Go!

1. Look around you and name 6 things in nature. Make sure you have a mixture of plants, animals, insects, and nonliving items. Example: bird, fish, ant, tree, flower, sun. Draw one picture on each paper or card, naming each. (On the 7th card, let child draw a picture of himself/herself.)

2. Shuffle cards and match any two together. Tell how the pictures are similar and different. Examples:

Tree + fish How are a tree and fish alike?
(Both need water to live)
How are they different?
(Tree can't swim; fish has no leaves)

Flower + sun How are they alike?
(Both can be yellow)
How are they different?
(Flower lives in earth, sun in sky)

Bird + child How are you and a bird alike?
(Have eyes and feet, eat and drink)
How are you different?
(I can't fly, bird can't read books)

Let's talk

Are you like everything on your cards?
Are you different from everything on your cards?
Think of someone you know who has a different skin color. How
   are you alike? How are you different?
If everything on Earth is alike and different, does that mean we're
   all related?

Same and Different

Find the differences in similar natural forms

The Inside Scoop: Our world is built upon the opposites of *sameness* and *difference*; the duality and diversity of nature arising out of its productive unity. Differences are found in sameness. During a blizzard, all snowflakes look alike, but, examined individually, each snowflake has a uniquely different design. Corn stalks in a field look identical to a passerby, but each plant has a different pattern of leaf and tassel growth. In humans, identical twins may fool teachers and friends, but each individual exhibits unique talents, habits, and peculiarities.

Get ready!   Magnifying glass

Get set!   Point out common objects that have the same name but are different in some way.
Examples:
> Two untied sneakers are the same, until a bow is tied on one. They are still the *same* (sneakers), but *different* (one tied, one untied)
> Two T-shirts are the same, but may have different logos or colors
> Two hands are the same, but one may be clean and the other dirty

Go!   1. Find two natural objects outdoors that generally look alike—then look closely to find the differences. (Make the difference very obvious. You might start with two very dissimilar leaves, then

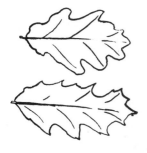

pair two leaves from the same tree. Match flower heads, pine cones, shells, etc.

2. If animals or insects are present in groups or pairs, try to point out how they are the same and yet different.

Let's talk

Look down at your feet. Are they the same? How can you make them different? Are they still feet after you've made them different?

How would you feel if everything in the world was exactly the same?

How are you the same as every person in the world? How are you different?

GUIDED IMAGERY
In a
Bubble

Experience the sensations of a trip above the Earth.

Narrator: Have the children sit or lie down. Read slowly, with feeling.

Let's get comfortable . . . close your eyes . . . and try to see and feel my words. Are you ready?

Imagine you're in the middle of a shimmering bubble . . . a gleaming rainbow sphere . . . floating over the blue-green ocean . . . lifted by currents of warm air as the sun heats the water . . . bouncing daintily on island breezes . . . over palm trees and white sandy beaches where sea turtles lay their eggs . . . and shells wash in-and-out with the waves.

Up, up you float : . . . rolling and rocking in a strong gust of wind . . . over land dotted with green forests and snowy mountain peaks. . . where bear cubs trail behind their mothers . . . and hawks glide and soar beside you. The air is colder, but you're protected in your warm bubble . . . so clear that you can see in every direction . . . land and rivers, sky and clouds.

Tumbling, rolling over cornfields and pastures where horses gallop and prance . . . over steamy jungles where monkeys dangle from trees . . . and red-and-green parrots squawk noisily . . . over dry deserts . . . careful! Don't let that prickly cactus pop your bubble! Float high over skyscrapers and mile-long bridges . . . see the people below— rushing, scurrying to work and school . . . while pigeons and squirrels, bees and bats, go about their busy work . . . living quietly among people . . . wildlife and people living together in one space.

Float over seas and land, mountains and ice packs . . . where brown, white, yellow, and red people speak German, French, Chinese, Hindi, English . . . wearing saris, trousers, robes, or nothing at all. Rise up high over the pretty blue-and-white ball called Earth . . . shining against the black sky . . . and look down . . . see trees and grass and rocks, bears and hawks and pigeons, people of all colors . . . living together . . . on one lovely planet.

Appendix A
Flow Learning Method

What is Flow Learning™?

A natural, flexible method of *teaching*

. . . allowing you to *mix and match* activities

. . . in a *purposeful, directional* way

. . . for an *endless variety* of nature experiences.

Designed by naturalist Joseph Cornell, the Flow Learning™ model has an impressive 20-year history of providing successful indoor/outdoor learning experiences in varied situations, with groups of many nationalities, ages and backgrounds.

Based on fundamental principles of human behavior and motivation, Flow Learning™ takes young people from action to awareness to reflection. A non-rigid grouping of activities, games, and stories shows children *how* to think—not *what* to think—while exploring the home they share with all other living things.

Youth group leaders, naturalists, home-schooling parents, and other educators will find that Flow Learning™ not only simplifies environmental education programming and lesson planning but also allows freedom to respond to the needs and circumstances of the moment.

Parents, grandparents, and day-care providers can provide a spontaneous "learn without teaching" experience by following the same pattern outlined for professional educators.

Flow Learning™ mirrors the cycle inherent in human behavior to help you plan a balanced, stimulating, FUN experience for children of all ages! Flow Learning™ has four stages that "flow" from one into another:

Awaken Enthusiasm → Focus Attention → Direct Experience → Share Inspiration

Parents and teachers will recognize this same pattern recurring in the daily lives and activities of their own young children:

Play   **Sense**   **Do**   **Listen**
(Action) → (Observation) → (Work) → (Rest)

Here is how Joseph Cornell in *Sharing the Joy of Nature* describes the four stages, their qualities and benefits:

Stage One: *Awaken Enthusiasm* [Otter]

Quality: Playfulness & alertness
Benefits:

- Builds on children's love of play
- Creates an atmosphere of enthusiasm
- A dynamic beginning gets everyone saying "Yes!"
- Develops full alertness, overcomes passivity
- Creates involvement
- Gets attention (minimizes discipline problems)
- Develops rapport with the leader
- Creates good group dynamics
- Provides direction and structure
- Prepares for later, more sensitive activities

Stage Two: *Focus Attention* [Crow]

Quality: Receptivity
Benefits:

- Increases attention span
- Deepens awareness by focusing attention
- Positively channels enthusiasm generated in Stage One
- Develops observational skills
- Calms the mind
- Develops receptivity for more sensitive nature experiences

Stage Three: *Direct Experience* [Bear]

Quality: Absorption
Benefits:

- People learn best by personal discovery
- Gives direct, experiential, intuitive understanding
- Fosters wonder, empathy and love
- Develops personal commitment to ecological ideals

Stage Four: *Share Inspiration* [Dolphin]

Quality: Idealism
Benefits:

- Clarifies and strengthens personal experiences
- Builds on uplifted mood
- Introduces inspiring role models
- Gives peer reinforcement
- Creates group bonding
- Provides feedback for the leader
- Leader can share inspiration with a receptive audience

All of the activities in this book are listed here, under the stages of Flow Learning™ for which they can be used most effectively. Use this chart to help you design your Flow Learning™ sessions.

Stage One: *Awaken Enthusiasm*
(Key words: High-energy, playful, running, crawling, digging, noisy, messy)

Backwards Day

Claws, Paws & Thumbs

Coats of Many Colors

Earth Pizza

Egg Toss

Forks in the Road

Frosty the Birdman

Magic Square

Oh, Nuts!

Rock Art

Seed Socks

Shadow Play

Snake Slithers

Sun Trap

Trick or Trash

Stage Two: *Focus Attention*
(Key words: Receptive, aware, observing, quiet, calm, smell, tasting, feeling, touching)

Animal Toons

Barefoot Hiking

Beginnings and Endings

Butterflight

Crepuscular Critters

Home Sweet Home

No See'ums

Nose Hike

Picture Me

Say My Way

Skyglow

Snag Hotel

Snoring Snapdragons

Spiral Sprouts

Spishing

Starlight Stories

Tree Talk

Who Am I?

Stage Three: *Direct Experience*
(Key words: Absorbed, busy, curious, working, sorting, doing, discovering, experimenting)

Cereal Stones

Don't Bug Me

Drought Garden

Home Improvement

Wee World

Leaf Lines

Locomotion

Lumps and Bumps

Moon Illusion

My Body Is the World

Name Game

Pack It Out

Prickles

Rooty-Toot-Toot

Same and Different

Spore Prints

The Unhuggables

Stage Four: *Share Inspiration*
(Key words: Listening, reflection, thoughtful, ideas, ideals, love, bonding, feedback)

Poems:
Fat Garden Blues
Tree Hotel
Down Under My Feet
I Spy Animal Eyes
The Unscary Scarecrow
A Week at Camp
A Meteor Shower
Play Lightly on the Earth

Guided Imagery:
Growing Toward the Sun
In the Forest
Journey to the Center of the Earth
Hiding from the Storm
In a Bird's Nest
Floating Downstream
Across the Galaxy
In a Bubble

Sample Flow Learning™ Session
(Single Theme: Wildlife World)

Stage One: Awaken Enthusiasm with "Oh, Nuts!"

Stage Two: Focus Attention with "Who Am I?"

Stage Three: Direct Experience with "Don't Bug Me"

Stage Four: Share Inspiration with "I Spy Animal Eyes"

Sample Flow Learning™ Session
(Mixed Theme: Human/One World/Plant)

Stage One: Awaken Enthusiasm with "Claws, Paws & Thumbs"

Stage Two: Focus Attention with "Picture Me"

Stage Three: Direct Experience with "Leaf Lines"

Stage Four: Share Inspiration with "Growing Toward the Sun"

Appendix B
Adapting Activities for Indoor Use

Is there a blizzard raging outside? Lightning flashing across the sky? Is it 105 degrees in the shade? While severe weather conditions make great learning experiences, it's safer to keep youngsters inside.

All activities in this book are designed for outdoor exploration; however, the following activities can be adapted for indoor use.

Plants

Activity	Special Needs for Indoors
Leaf Lines	Variety of freshly-picked leaves
Lumps & Bumps	Goldenrod stalks with galls, or other types of galls
Prickles	Any prickly house plant, e.g. cactus; or teasels, cuttings of rose or raspberry canes
Rooty-Toot-Toot	Two different samples of root systems
Spiral Sprouts	Cuttings of branches showing 3 different growing patterns
Spore Prints	Assortment of gilled mushrooms

Wildlife

Activity	Special Needs for Indoors
Animal Toons	Pictures of wildlife and their "homes"
Don't Bug Me	Captured bugs
Locomotion	Captured bugs
Snake Slithers	(None)
The Unhuggables	Domesticated animals; toy animals
Who Am I?	Pictures of wildlife to pantomime

Birds

Activity	Special Needs for Indoors
Egg Toss	Weeds, leaves, grass clippings, brush, other outdoor nesting material
Home Improvement	Small twigs, dried grass, feathers, other soft nesting material

Humans

Activity	Special Needs for Indoors
Backwards Day	(None)
Claws, Paws & Thumbs	Variety of natural items (both easy and difficult to pick up "thumbless"), e.g. stones, acorns, twigs w/leaves or berries, shells, etc.

All Together

Activity	Special Needs for Indoors
Beginnings & Endings	Variety of natural items in stages of birth and death, e.g. empty bird's egg, flower or leaf bud, dandelion puffball, dried leaf, seeds, sprouts, dead bugs (Remember: often the *ending* of one cycle is the *beginning* of another)
Home Sweet Home	Pictures of various outdoor environments, e.g. desert, shore, meadow, mountain, snowfield
Magic Square	Enough natural items to fit a selected theme area
My Body Is the World	Posters of natural forms that have similarities to the human form, e.g. tree, flower
Picture Me	(None)
Same and Different	Pairs of natural objects with subtle differences

NOTE: All of the Poetry and Guided Imagery may be read and discussed either indoors or out.

Glossary

abdomen The hindmost of the three main body divisions of insects.

acid rain Air pollution formed by the reaction of water in the air with chemicals given off as waste, mostly by factories and cars.

aerate To supply with air or oxygen.

camouflage Blending in with the surroundings to avoid detection.

cavity A hole in a tree.

community A group of plants and animals that live in one particular area.

crepuscular Active at dawn and dusk.

cross section The view of the tree you get by cutting across, or perpendicular to, the length of the tree.

crustaceans A group of animals which includes crabs, lobsters, shrimps, prawns, and barnacles.

decomposer A plant or animal that feeds on dead materials and causes their breakdown.

diurnal Day-active.

ecosystem The combination of living things (e.g., plants and animals) and nonliving things (e.g., soil, water, air) in an area.

fibrous root system Roots with many branchings, all somewhat alike in length and diameter, which do not penetrate the soil as deeply as taproots (e.g., grass).

fungi Organisms such as mold, yeast, and mushrooms that feed on living things (such as tree roots and leaves) or dead organic matter.

gall An abnormal growth on a plant, sometimes caused by an insect.

habitat An area that provides food, water, and shelter for an animal.

insectivore An animal that mainly eats insects.

larva An immature insect that looks completely different from the adult insect (e.g., a caterpillar or a maggot).

microhabitat A very small area that provides food, water, and shelter.

mushroom The part of a fungus that produces spores, which spread the fungus to other areas.

nocturnal	Night-active.
organic matter	Chemical compounds of carbon and other elements, produced in the life processes of plants and animals, and a source of food for bacteria.
organism	A living thing.
predator	An animal that eats another animal, known as the *prey*.
prey	An animal that is eaten by another animal, known as the *predator*.
rays	The part of the tree that stores food and transports food across the rings to the bark.
scat	Animal droppings.
seedling	A young tree that is less than waist high.
skyglow	A city's glow on the horizon caused by excessive artificial lighting.
snag	A dead tree that is still standing.
species	A basic grouping of living things that are similar to each other and can breed with each other to produce offspring which themselves can breed together.
spore	A microscopic reproductive cell produced without sexual fusion, usually from fungi, mosses, or ferns.
symmetry	The similarity of form on either side of a dividing line. The opposite sides are a balanced match.
taproot	The main root, growing vertically downward, from which small branch roots spread out (e.g., carrot).
territory	An area defended by an animal against others of the same species.
thorax	The middle body segment of an insect, to which the legs and wings are attached.
tree ring	The circular band laid down each year by a growing tree. The number of tree rings indicates the age of the tree, and their widths indicate how fast the tree has been growing.
wildlife	Animals that are not tamed or domesticated. Wildlife includes insects, spiders, birds, reptiles, fish, amphibians, and mammals.

Index of Activities
By Main Topic

Evidence of Wildlife
Crepuscular Critters; Lumps and Bumps; No See'ums; Snag Hotel

Habitat Components
Home Improvement; Home Sweet Home; Wee World; Snag Hotel

Human/Wildlife Relationship
Animal Toons; Butterflight; Frosty the Birdman; Spishing; The Unhuggables; Who Am I?

Interdependence
Earth Pizza; Home Sweet Home; Lumps and Bumps; Magic Square; Picture Me; Seed Socks

Language Skills
Animal Toons; Backwards Day; Barefoot Hiking; Beginnings and Endings; Home Sweet Home; Picture Me; Say My Way; Starlight Stories

Navigation
Backwards Day; Butterflight; Locomotion; Oh Nuts; Snake Slithers

Patterns/Symmetry
Butterflight; Leaf Lines; My Body Is the World; Same and Different; Spiral Sprouts; Starlight Stories

Pollution
Pack It Out; Skyglow; Snag Hotel; Trick or Trash

Protection
Egg Toss; Home Improvement; Lumps and Bumps; Pack It Out; Prickles; Shadow Play

Responsibility
Pack It Out; Trick or Trash

Sensation/Perception
Backwards Day; Barefoot Hiking; Claws, Paws & Thumbs; Nose Hike; Say My Way

Soil and Water
Cereal Stones; Drought Garden; Earth Pizza; Rooty-Toot-Toot

Temperature
Barefoot Hiking; Sun Trap

Usefulness
Claws, Paws & Thumbs; Forks in the Road; Wee World; Moon Illusion; Tree Talk

ENJOY OTHER DISTINCTIVE NATURE AWARENESS BOOKS FROM DAWN PUBLICATIONS . . .

Sharing Nature with Children, Joseph Cornell's now-classic collection of original nature games. More than 380,000 sold in nine languages! Now in a significantly expanded and enhanced second edition (Spring 1998).

Sharing the Joy of Nature, in which Joseph Cornell introduces more nature games and explains his remarkable Flow Learning technique.

Journey to the Heart of Nature, Joseph Cornell's guide to an in-depth exploration of a personally selected place in nature, along with many stories of great nature explorers.

Listening to Nature, by Joseph Cornell, a beautiful book that transports adults into the quiet mystery of nature. Stunning photographs and profound commentary makes this a favorite of many.

. . . AND DAWN'S PICTURE BOOKS FOR CHILDREN

The Dandelion Seed, by Joseph Anthony, follows a seed through a lifelong journey filled with exploration, challenges and fulfillment, a metaphor for us all.

Places of Power, by Michael DeMunn, reveals the places of power that native people all over the world have always known, and how to let your place of power speak to your open heart.

Wonderful Nature, Wonderful You, by Karin Ireland, explores the lessons of nature and finds their relevance for us all.

Walking with Mama, by Barbara Stynes, portrays the sweet intimacy a mother and child share when walking together in nature.

Lifetimes, by David Rice, introduces some of nature's longest, shortest, and most unusual lifetimes—and each one's message for us. This book teaches, but also goes right to the heart.

The Tree in the Ancient Forest, by Carol Reed-Jones, reveals in cumulative verse the remarkable interdependent web of plants and animals living around a single old fir tree.

A Swim through the Sea, A Walk in the Rainforest, and *A Fly in the Sky*, a trilogy by Kristin Joy Pratt, are three joyful, illustrated tours of some of Earth's most important biospheres.

Discover the Seasons, by Diane Iverson, introduces the young child to the wonders of changing seasons in verse, plus seasonally appropriate activities and recipes.

Teachers: ask about our *Sharing Nature with Children Series* of teacher's guides by Bruce and Carol Malnor—a practical and creative way to incorporate Dawn's books into the school curriculum. Ask also for information about school visits by our authors and illustrators.

Dawn Publications is dedicated to inspiring in children a deeper understanding and appreciation for all life on Earth. For a copy of our catalog please call 800-545-7475. Please also visit our web site at www.dawnpub.com.